Manuscript Alphabet

Aa Bb Cc Dd Ee

Ff Gg Hh Ii Jj

Kk Ll Mm Nn

Oo Pp Qq Rr

Ss Tt Uu V

Ww Xx Yy Z

1

Aa

Adam

alligator

Anna was amazed to see an alligator in Adam's aquarium.

3

Bobby
bubbles

b

B

Bobby Baboon blew bubbles
beside the bus.

CARNIVAL

crawled

Candice

C c

C

6

Candice Caterpillar crawled to the carnival for cotton candy.

delicious

Duke

d

D

Duke Dog ate dozens of delicious doughnuts.

elephant

Elle

e

E

Ellie Elephant eats an eggplant every evening.

fireworks

Felicia

Ff

Ff

12

Felicia Flamingo saw fireworks at the fair.

gorilla

Ginger

Gg

G

Ginger Gorilla gobbled a
gallon of green grapes.

hopscotch

luau

h

H

16

Hannah Hen happily played hopscotch in Hawaii.

Welcome to IRELAND

Iguana

Ingrid

I

I

Ingrid Iguana ate ice cream on the island of Ireland.

Welcome to
IRELAND

Jelly fish

Jocelyn

f

f f

Jocelyn the jazzy jellyfish just loved her job as a jeweler.

Kittens

Ken

King Ken kept kittens and
koalas in the kitchen.

lollipops

lots

Lots of ladybugs licked
lollipops in the long car.

muffins

Martin

m

M

Martin Monkey rode his
motorcycle in the mountains
while munching muffins.

necktie

Nina

n

N

28

Nina noticed her nice neighbor's nifty new necktie.

opposum

Oliver

o

O

Oliver Opposum offered
oranges to owls in outer space.

popcorn

patrick

P p

P p

Patrick Pelican purchased popcorn from the pig in the park.

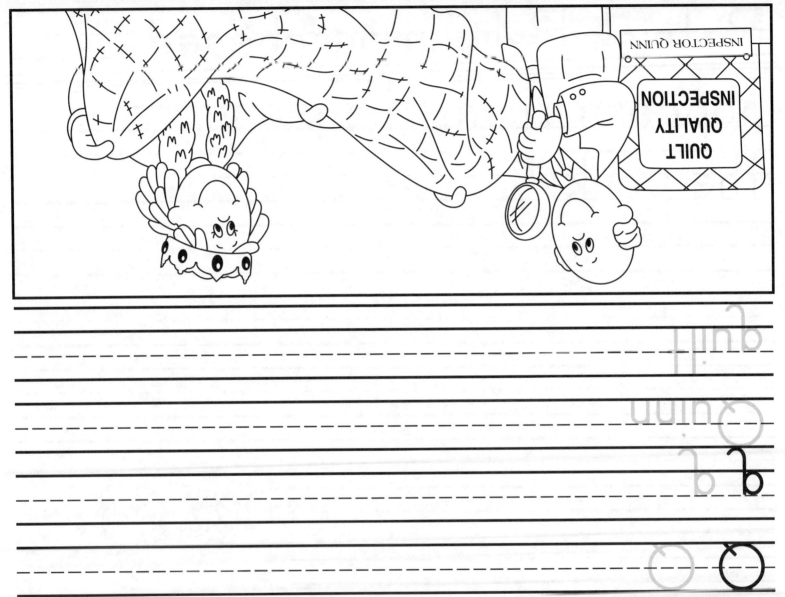

34

Quinn questioned the quality
of the queen's quaint quilt.

recover

Richard

r

R

Richard Rhino raced down the
rocky ridge to recover the
radio.

sunset

Samantha

s s

S S

Samantha Snail sang softly as she sailed into the sunset.

Truck

Terry

T t

T t

40

Terry Tiger's toy truck transformed into a T. rex.

Umbrella

Ulysses

u

U

42

The players rushed to get under Ulysses' umbrella to keep their uniforms dry.

Vacation

Vivian

V

V

44

Vivian Vulture visited a variety of vacation spots.

VENICE

Watermelon

Walter

W

W

46

Walter Walrus weighed watermelons on Wednesday.

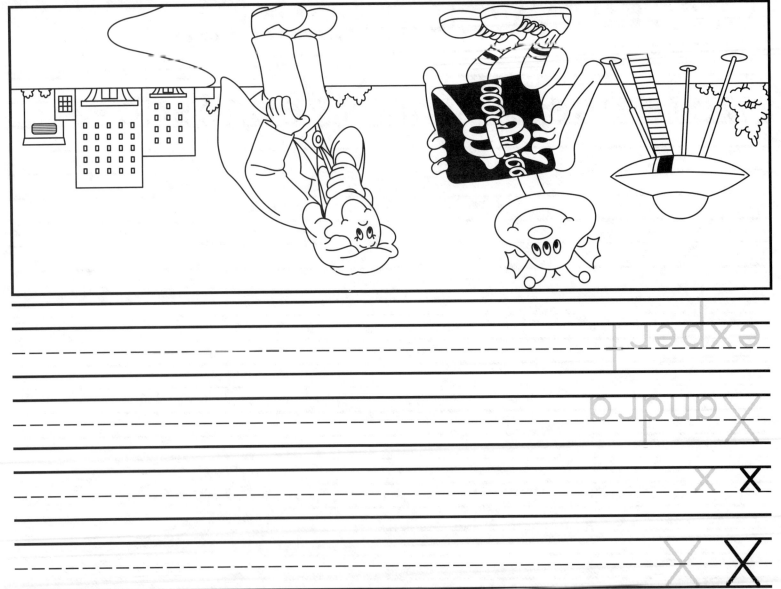

expert

Xandra

X

X

48

Xandra the expert excitedly examined the x-ray.

Yolanda

Y Y

Yesterday, Yolanda yodeled "yoo-hoo" to Yvonne.

ZOO

Zz

Zz

Zack

zipped

Zack Zebra zipped through the zinnias at the zoo.

Trace and write the numbers and number words.

0 zero

1 one

2 two

3 three

4 four

5 five

6 six

7 seven

8 eight

9 nine

10 ten

Trace and write the days of the week.

Sunday

Monday

Tuesday

Wednesday

Thursday

Friday

Saturday

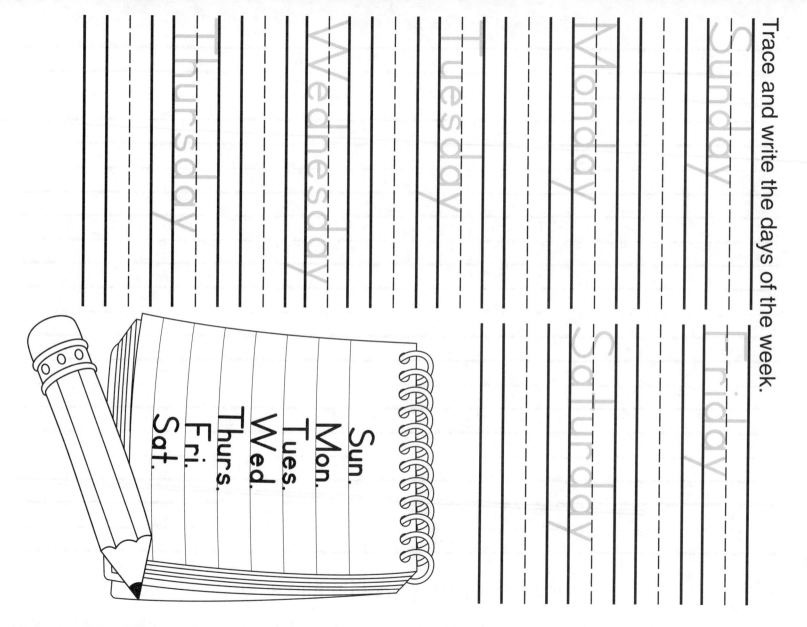

Sun.
Mon.
Tues.
Wed.
Thurs.
Fri.
Sat.

Trace and write the months of the year on the lines below.

January   February

March   April

May   June

July

Trace and write the months of the year on the lines below.

August   September

October   November

December

Finish the sentences.

My friends and I like to
_____
_____

I laugh when
_____
_____

Last night I saw
_____
_____

Finish the sentences.

When I am playing, I

When I grow up,

My favorite vacation is

Pretend you are going to the grocery store. Use the words in the word box to make a list of some foods you would buy for breakfast, lunch, and dinner.

pancakes	corn	peanut butter
doughnuts	cake	beets
soup	spaghetti	tacos
butter	cereal	waffles
eggs	bread	apples
milk	cookies	jelly
orange	macaroni	lettuce
juice	tomatoes	ice cream
pizza	pie	cheese
hot dogs		
muffins		
celery		
bananas		
chicken		
green beans		
potatoes		
rice		
steak		

Breakfast

_____

- - - - - - - - - - - - - - -

_____

- - - - - - - - - - - - - - -

_____

_____

- - - - - - - - - - - - - - -

_____

- - - - - - - - - - - - - - -

_____

_____

- - - - - - - - - - - - - - -

_____

_____

Lunch

Dinner

Imagine you can have any ice cream treat you want! Use the words in the word box to write about your favorite treat.

banana split	cookie dough	peanuts	sprinkles
butterscotch	custard	raisins	strawberry
caramel	frozen	ripple	sundae
cherry	fudge	sandwich	syrup
chocolate	marshmallow	scoops	vanilla
cone	milkshake	sherbet	whipped cream

Have you been to the zoo? Use the words in the word box to write about the animals you have seen, or would like to see.

chimpanzee	emu	ostrich	monkey
peacock	dolphin	parrot	giraffe
polar bear	snake	owl	zebra
gorilla	lizard	bear	lion
leopard	turtle	shark	tiger
flamingo	duck	otter	elephant

Birthdays are your special days. Use the words in the word box to write about your best birthday ever, or write what you would like to do on your next birthday.

birthday	balloons	friends	pony	paint
cake	ice cream	fun	dance	crafts
party	clown	play	color	food
candles	puppet	happy	neighbors	family
presents	snacks	wish	streamers	pizza
games	toys	surprise	party hats	prizes

Great Books For Small Business . . .

The Greatest Little Business Book
The Essential Guide to Starting a Small Business

A comprehensive, yet readable, reference book. A best-seller and highl[y] recommended by small business advisers. Many worked examples, eg Cashflo[w] Forecast, Business Plan and a Partnership Agreement. Also: legalitie[s] raising finance, finding premises, employing staff, tax & VAT. Update[d] annually. 120 pages with many illustrations. by **Peter Hingston** **£7.5[0]**

The Greatest Sales & Marketing Book
The Practical Action Guide for a Small Business

Full of ideas to increase your sales. How to advertise successfully. Many worke[d] examples, eg Pricing, a Press Release and Leaflet. Tips to survive a Recessio[n] Hints to avoid losing sales. Advice to keep down overheads. Market Research how to do it and how it helps. The book has had many excellent reviews, f[or] example, *The Times, Money Week* and *British Business* magazine. Update[d] regularly. 120 pages and highly illustrated. by **Peter Hingston** **£7.5[0]**

The Greatest Guide to Home-based Business
101 Great Business Ideas plus How to Work from Home

Working from home is the growth area of new businesses in the 1990s. Th[is] book is co-authored by Eric Smith, Australia's leading author on small busine[ss] subjects. In addition to advice on starting a business in Britain, it covers t[he] particular problems of working from home. The book also features 101 gre[at] business ideas to inspire the reader.
120 pages and illustrated. by **Peter Hingston & Eric Smith** **£7.[**

The Best Accounts Books
For non-VAT (and VAT) registered Small Businesses

These accounts books were launched in late 1991 and are fast becoming cl[ass] leaders. Written in layman's language, with a simple and attractive format a[nd] full instructions. Suitable for most businesses (sole traders, partnerships limited companies). Choose between the YELLOW BOOK (for a *cash* busine[ss] or the BLUE BOOK (for a *credit* business). A4 size, hardcover. **£7.[**

The BLUE BOOK is also available in a VAT version with extra columns for VAT, a complete VAT Section and help to complete your VAT Returns. **£9.[**

HOW TO ORDER

From a Bookshop: Take this to any bookshop and ask them to order the book from [us] through Teleordering. We usually despatch within 2-3 days. Trade terms.

By Mail Order: Either phone us with your credit card details, or send a cheque (made [to] Hingston Associates). For post & packing, add **£1** per guide book, **£1.25** for non-V[AT] accounts books and **£1.50** for VAT accounts books. Allow about 7 days for delivery.

Hingston Associates, Westlands House, Tullibardine, Auchterarder, Perthshire PH3 1N[
Tel: 0764 662058

The Greatest Little Busin k

The Essential Guide to Starting a Small Business

Written by Peter Hingston

Illustrations, cartoons and graphic design by Charlotte Hingston

Copyright © 1993 by Peter Hingston. All rights reserved. 6th Edition. Reprinted: 1994 with minor updates.

Previous editions: Copyright © 1985, 1987, 1988, 1990, 1991.
Revised/Reprinted 1986, 1987, 1988, 1989, 1992.
Foreign language editions: Polish (1992), Ukrainian (1994), Hungarian (1994).

Published by Hingston Associates,
Westlands House, Tullibardine, by Auchterarder, Perthshire PH3 1NJ, U.K.
Telephone: 0764 662058   Fax: 0764 662382.

Printed in Great Britain by Hobbs the Printers of Southampton.

ISBN 0 906555 13 2

Introduction

I hope you will find this a most useful book — I only wish there had been such a book when I first started in business! I have tried to write it to be clear, readable and full of practical information.

The first edition was written in 1985 when I was Director of a Local Enterprise Agency providing advice to people setting up in business and I could not find a suitable book for my clients. The book therefore tries to answer precisely the sort of questions people ask when they are thinking of starting a business. It also points out the many things which people do not ask about but which they do need to know.

As your time is short, please don't feel you have to read the book from cover to cover, just dip into the section which is of immediate interest.

If you have not already made contact with your Local Enterprise Agency or business development unit, remember they are there to help you and much of their advice is free. Refer to the last chapter in this book to find your nearest Agency.

I wish you every success with your new venture.

Peter Hingston

Acknowledgements

Charlotte Hingston	For all the illustrations, cartoons and the layout of the book together with suggestions for the text, proof reading and the encouragement necessary to complete this project.
Jimmy Walker	For detailed analysis and comprehensive suggestions for the text.

In addition I am indebted to the following who read sections, chapters or complete draft manuscripts and who provided many suggestions which have been incorporated in the final version. (Appointments are as of Summer 1985 when the first edition was written).

Fred Brooksbank	Scottish Development Agency
Elizabeth Cameron	Inverclyde Enterprise Trust Ltd
Craig Campbell	Arthur Young, Glasgow
John Carpenter	Milton Keynes Business Venture
Robert Colvil	R. W. Colvil & Co
Edward Cunningham	Scottish Development Agency
Eric Firth	Welsh Walker & Co
Tom Ford	Colchester Business Enterprise Agency
Dick Glover	Industrial Relations & Personnel Consultants Ltd
David Hingston	Procurator Fiscal, Wick
John Jacobs	Edinburgh Venture Enterprise Trust
Joanna James	3i, Edinburgh
Don Kennedy	Small Firms Service, Glasgow
David Lochtie	Thomas Bryce Insurance
Roger Massey	Strathclyde Microsystems Centre
Lilian Morris	
George Paterson	Glasgow Opportunities
Mac Robertson	
William Smith	Campbell Smith Insurance
A.J. Stewart	Industry Department for Scotland
George Stewart	Royal Bank of Scotland plc
Jack Thomson	Woodrow & Thomson

Cover Photographs: M. Lungley (Blacksmith), C. Donaldson (Ceramics).

My thanks to Gerry Quigley, Chairman of the Inverclyde Enterprise Trust Ltd for his permission to use the Trust's IBM PC computer on which the original text was typed in 1985.

Additional Acknowledgements for the 4th Edition: Don Kennedy of Business Information Services, Roger Harvey of Willow Typesetting.
Additional Acknowledgements for the 6th Edition: Peter Bevan, Federation of Small Businesses, Irene Goodall, Perth & Kinross Environmental Health Department, Scottish Business Shop, Tayside Trading Standards Department.

Contents

Thinking of a Business Idea

The very first stage in setting up a business is to think of what type of business it might be, in other words to get a business "idea". At first glance it may appear that this is purely a matter of inspiration with the lucky entrepreneur waking up in the middle of the night with the great idea that will make him or her a millionaire! That might actually happen on the odd occasion but it is rare. Other people think of setting up in business doing what they have done in the past as an employee. This isn't necessarily the best approach either — instead you should be asking yourself "just what is it that people want?".

The lucky entrepreneur waking up in the middle of the night ...

This chapter is for those readers who are thinking of setting up in business but who have not yet thought of what they are going to do. Here are some of the techniques that people use to come up with a business idea:

Copying This is probably the most common way a business idea is conceived. In essence it works like this — you might see a product or service which is not available locally so you could fill the gap by introducing it to your area. Almost every shop is an example of this, but there are many other possible examples — leisure industry activities, local magazines etc.

To get such an idea you could visit another area (if outside London, you can pick up good ideas by a one-week visit to the capital) or better still, if you can afford it, visit the Continent or North America. The last destination is a rich source of business ideas and products which are not yet available in this country — just walk the streets, look around the shops, watch the TV commercials and read the papers and magazines to get lots of ideas. Of course not everything that is a success abroad would necessarily be such a success in this country.

One form of copying that is not recommended is to simply mimic another established business and to set up in direct competition.

Franchising This is similar to "Copying" as mentioned above except you do it with the full support of the business you are copying under an agreement called a "franchise". In this the franchise giver (called the "franchisor") allows you to use his name and get his expertise with all its benefits. In exchange you as the "franchisee" have

to pay the franchisor for the benefit of using his name and obtaining his advice but the major advantage is that it allows the new entrepreneur to get into business more quickly with less of the risks that normally exist. This is an important enough technique to merit a section of its own later in this chapter.

Buying An Existing Business This is another popular means for acquiring a business idea, and in fact, shortcuts much of the start-up process. But its very ease belies the possible pitfalls and many a retired or newly redundant person has lost all his or her money buying a shop, pub, sub-post office or small hotel. It is an important subject and is covered in a separate section later in this chapter.

Product Spin-Off This is where a designer while working on one product might realise that a variant of that product has quite a different use and so he sets up his own business to exploit that. Alternatively he or she might think of a significant improvement to an existing product which, if it was to go into production, would take a good share of the market. (Legal advice may be required to ensure you do not infringe any patents etc).

Arts & Crafts This applies mainly to those with a formal training in arts and crafts or who have some unusually good talent. It must be admitted that trying to start a profitable business based on your arts or crafts talents is very difficult for many complex reasons — one of which is the problem of distributing your product widely enough through many outlets. Again there are exceptions but you have to identify a

Thinking of a Business Idea

real market need which is large enough to provide you with a living wage. You also need to know how to promote and distribute your products and allocate enough time for this in addition to your creative work.

Inventions There is a widespread belief that you have to invent something before you can start a manufacturing business. The fact is that few businesses start this way and though some have been enormously successful it is not an easy path to tread. In Britain only about 2% of patented inventions are now by private individuals, the remainder being filed by companies and government research departments.

One might think the biggest problem is designing the new device but in fact that is the least of it for the main problem is selling it to a generally disbelieving public who are naturally conservative and wary of new things. To launch an innovative product requires substantial promotional or advertising budgets. Also, of every 10 new product ideas only one is ever likely to go into production.

Personal Experience This is often a good way to stumble onto business ideas, a personal experience having revealed a market gap. For instance, you might have difficulty in obtaining say, a book that gives you all the essential advice you need to lay out a new garden and if you find that other people have the same problem then you might consider writing one!

Or, when you are trying to sell something, the customer might reply *"We don't really want that, but what we really need desperately and cannot get is a (something else)"*. This approach

Patents Relate to products, processes, mechanisms, materials etc. To be patentable an invention must be: 1. new; 2. involve an inventive step and 3. be capable of industrial application. Advisable to contact a registered Patent Agent at an early stage (see Yellow Pages).

Registered Designs Relate to the looks or style of a product. Is judged solely by eye. Only the appearance given by an object's actual shape, configuration, pattern or ornament can be protected, not an underlying idea. Again, best to contact a Patent Agent.

Warning: If you wish to apply for a patent or registered design, contact a Patent Agent *before* publicly disclosing your invention (or design) as such disclosure forfeits your protection.

Reg'd Trade & Service Marks Relate to a symbol or word or combination that distinguishes the products (or service) of a particular business. It provides protection for the goodwill and reputation of a firm. Handled by Patent Agent or Trade Mark Agent.

Copyright Relates to printed matter, music, works of art, architecture, films, computer programs etc. 3-D articles now have "Design Right" protection where based on a designer's drawings. In the UK no registration is required but vital to have proof of date. Protection is automatic and immediate. May be advisable to use the copyright symbol © etc.

Note You cannot protect a business idea, only something physical.

often prompts very good sales leads as it reveals what the customer really wants rather than what you thought he wanted. The good salesman would then ask his next customer *"Do you ever need a (whatever)?"* and if the answer is similar to the first customer and confirmed by others then he has probably found a good business idea.

Hobbies/Sports Sometimes there are business opportunities that can arise from your hobby or sport. In this situation, success requires the entrepreneur to have a fair amount of experience in the sport or activity to know what is required. In particular, many good sportsmen and women use their talents to make money outside their sport but related to it. For instance, golf professionals open golf shops. Their experience allows them to know what products to stock, their fame can be used to get publicity for the enterprise and their advice will be appreciated by customers. But a word of caution — some people involved in hobbies or sports dabble in selling something related to their activity but which will earn little more than pin money. There is a risk with this approach to business ideas that people start a business more for their love of the sport or hobby rather than there being a clear market need which they can fill and which will give them a living.

In General
Your business idea will have a better chance of success if you can develop a "unique selling proposition", ie a product or service that customers cannot obtain elsewhere. This does not require the whole business to be unique but you must offer something that is different, which could be the style of your service, the manner in which you package your products etc.

FRANCHISING

A Success Story Statistics which record the failure rate of new businesses vary depending upon the size of companies considered, the number of years before trading ceases and so on,

but without any dispute the figures all show a depressing picture. At least one in three of all new small businesses starting this year will not be trading in 3 year's time. Although fair comparative figures are hard to come by, it would appear that franchised new businesses in the UK have a better chance of surviving than the norm.

What Is Franchising? This is when an established business is prepared to sell you its image, its name, its business knowledge, its back up — in fact the whole proven business format. For any new business to be successful it needs a number of ingredients — a market for the product or service, the correct stock and tools, adequate finance and, most importantly, people with the actual skills to do the work and the necessary "business" knowledge (such as how to do the accounts). If any of these ingredients is weak or lacking, the chances of failure increase, so you can see why someone setting up in business for the first time (without a franchise) has to acquire a great deal of knowledge to survive and prosper.

In contrast, with a franchise operation, the business you take on is a well proven business idea and the professionals behind the franchise (called the "franchisors") should provide you (the "franchisee") with all the training and back-up you need to ensure you succeed. They are keen to see you prosper because they take a percentage of your takings (called a "royalty") and so their profitability is directly linked to your profitability. This is good insurance for you as you can be sure that they will maintain their interest in what you are doing!

Who Does Franchising? The type of franchising we are considering here is more correctly called "Business Format Franchising". Developed in the United States in the 1950s, many of the well-known franchise names are still American. In the United States one third of all retailing is done by franchise operations and it is a fast growing sector of the economy. In Britain franchising is becoming more familiar to people and there are now many hundreds of companies operating franchises, including some well-known names.

How Does Franchising Work In Practice? Setting up any business takes money, called "capital". With a franchise operation it costs you more, because you are paying for the business experience and proven product or service of the franchisor. In return he may set up the whole business for you — including the selection of premises, the associated legal work, the full training of yourself and finally, help you with selection of stock and/or tools. In some cases this "hand-holding" is so complete that the franchisor gets the premises completely ready and you are simply handed the keys to your own shop or fast-food outlet. While the premises are being found and prepared, the franchisor will be busy training you to run your new business.

What You Should Get In A Franchise

1. A proven business format.
2. The use of a business name/trademark.
3. The Operations Manual.
4. Training in both "trade" and business skills.
5. An exclusive territory.
6. Full support on start-up.
7. On-going advice and guidance.
8. Long-term market research to ensure your business keeps up with changes in the market place.
9. A contract clearly defining the rights and obligations of both parties.
10. Advertising support.
11. Trouble-shooting.

How To Assess A Franchise Operation

1. Get the franchisee information pack.
2. Visit the franchisor's head office.
3. Visit at least two of their franchisees (of your choice).
4. Assess several different franchises before choosing one.
5. Consult an accountant and solicitor before committing yourself.
6. Ask probing questions, such as:
   When was the business established?
   How many outlets are there in the UK?
   Who are the people behind the franchise?
   How good is the company's financial performance?
   What is the minimum capital required?
   What is the annual royalty charge?
   What do you get for your money?
   Are there other charges, eg advertising?
   What is the long-term for the product or service?
   Who is the competition?

Thinking of a Business Idea

When you start trading there is an Operations Manual which lays down the whole format of how to run the business — it is your "bible". In good franchise operations the franchisor works in close association with you to ensure you make good profits and run a sound business. This is in his own interest too as he will want a royalty, calculated as a fixed weekly or monthly amount or a percentage (2% to 20%) of your sales. Note that this royalty is usually based on your sales figure and not on your profits!

The rights and obligations of both parties are described in a contract which is a detailed document and forms the basis of the close association between yourself and the franchisor. Remember that contract law in Scotland and England are different so use a solicitor local to your area.

How To Find A Suitable Franchise
Many franchisors are members of the British Franchise Association (Thames View, Newtown Rd, Henley-on-Thames RG9 1HG. Tel: (0491) 578049). They provide an information pack (currently £17.50) for prospective franchisees, that includes a list of their members.

In addition, Franchise Development Services (Tel: Norwich (0603) 620301) publish the "Franchise Magazine" and the annual "UK Franchise Directory". The latter costs currently £25 and gives details of over 600 franchisors. There is also the "Franchise World Directory", currently £28.50, tel: 081-767 1371.

To meet franchisors, there are several major franchise Exhibitions held around the country (get details from the British Franchise Association). There is also a good book — "Taking Up A Franchise" written by Colin Barrow and Godfrey Golzen which is published by Kogan Page. Also, refer to the Box on the previous page and always consult an accountant and a solicitor before signing anything!

A Parting Shot If you want to start your own business and (a) do not know what to do, (b) have a reasonable amount of capital, say £5,000 minimum and (c) are not a loner who resents anyone being involved in your venture, then becoming a franchisee is one way to get into business. Prior experience of the trade that the franchise involves is usually not a requirement as franchisors prefer to instill their own methods during the training phase. Many successful franchisees are ex-executives or ex-forces personnel. A word of caution — taking on a franchise does not guarantee success as some have failed whilst others fail to meet projected turn-over figures. Even if successful, it will require much hard work and time for the business to become established.

Although there are certain constraints on being a franchisee such as you cannot adapt or modify the business or introduce sidelines, an important aspect of being in business for yourself, ie the amount of profit you can make, is mainly in your own hands.

BUYING AN EXISTING BUSINESS

This is a popular way for people to get into business for the first time and it can be successful, as it shortcuts much of the difficult start-up process. One learns of businesses for sale from adverts in "Daltons Weekly", local newspapers, from Business Transfer Agents (especially for shops) — see Yellow Pages and by word of mouth.

The Second-Hand Car Syndrome
Have you ever bought a second-hand car thinking you had bought just what you wanted, only to drive it home and discover it had so many faults you wished you had never seen it? Well, many people on being confronted with the opportunity to buy over another person's business often suffer the same experience so I have called it affectionately the "second-hand car syndrome". In the context of this book it often works something like this ..... Mr Smith was made redundant in his 50s but one day while talking to the proprietor of his local newsagent/general store, he learned that the store was up for sale as a going concern and he was flattered that the existing proprietor was prepared to offer the shop to him. Already the second-hand car syndrome was beginning to take effect as Mr Smith rushed home to tell his wife about the fantastic offer he had just been made. Mrs Smith was not so sure as she knew that the store was never busy when she was in it, the stock levels were low and the interior was rather run down and in need of a good refurbish. When she mentioned that to her husband he dismissed it saying that with some money spent on it he could increase the turnover "easily". Mrs Smith asked quietly if Mr Smith had asked the proprietor why he might be selling to which her husband replied the reason was due to ill health. Mrs Smith was unconvinced as she was contemplating the effect of the large supermarket that had opened up recently a few streets away.

One hopes that Mr Smith took professional advice from a surveyor and an accountant and indeed heeded their advice which was probably that the proprietor was now selling as the

Thinking of a Business Idea

business was declining due to the competition of the new supermarket. How can you stop yourself falling into the same trap? The answer is to do your homework thoroughly, to look carefully at the accounts, and to maintain an open yet cynical mind.

Why cynical? Because one must examine why a good small business is being sold. If the business is doing even reasonably well it is more likely to be taken over by a close friend, a member of the proprietor's family, or the proprietor could employ a manager. That is not to say that good or potentially good businesses do not come onto the market but the parallel to second-hand cars is close ... you need to know fully about what you are taking on and why it is being sold.

to put you in touch with a similar business probably far enough away not to be in direct competition. You will be surprised how many people will be quite happy to speak to you and impart good advice and hints. Also visit the local library and ask the librarian if there are any books on the subject, as many different types of business now have books written about them, sometimes written by people who have had to learn the hard way.

What Will It Cost?   This is not an easy question to answer as every business has its own strengths and weaknesses. However, in general terms a business has value due to its:

Stock   This is best valued independently (ie not by the seller). Remember all businesses suffer from "dead" stock

take into account their depreciated value.

Note: Depreciation is an accounting term which tries to put a life on an item. For instance, if the likely lifetime of a machine is 4 years, its value "depreciates" by 25% each year so if it cost £100 new, after a year its "accounts book" value would be £75, and after two years its value would be £75 less 25% and so on.

Machinery & Equipment   This is valued like Fixtures & Fittings.

Goodwill   Whereas the above categories can be valued precisely (it can still lead to disputes), goodwill is the really "grey" area of valuation. Goodwill equals the value of the Business less the tangible Business assets. It is a measure of the momentum of profitability that the business has built up. It should therefore be based on the proven profit of the business, looking at the last few years (since the business may be growing rapidly or declining). If a typical net profit (before tax) figure can be agreed on then the goodwill can be valued for a small business at usually between 1 and 5 times the profit figure. The actual multiplier chosen is dependent upon all the other factors involved in the sale, ie the perceived growth potential of the business, any patents or designs owned by the former business, the quality of staff and their training and the size of the existing customer base. Goodwill is very negotiable and if it relates closely to the former owner that part will be lost when he or she leaves and in that case it would be worth less!

The total value of the business, ie what you have to pay, is the sum of the four factors above of which the last is the most negotiable. Interestingly, the

Buying a business can be like buying a second-hand car.

Trade Knowledge   Do you know anything about the trade or the business you are contemplating taking over? If not, you are very vulnerable! Contact your local Enterprise Agency or business development unit (see the chapter **Getting more Business Advice**) for their advice and ask them

which is stock that is unlikely ever to be sold as it is either out-of-date, damaged or was never saleable in the first place! The valuation should therefore be the depreciated cost price (not retail price) of the saleable goods.

Fixtures & Fittings   Again this should be valued independently and it should

Thinking of a Business Idea

larger the business the greater the multiplier used when calculating the goodwill.

Financial Aspects Get advice from an accountant, who should go through the last few years accounts of the business and explain to you all the salient features. Be sure you also understand any tax implications of the purchase and you may also need to read a copy of the VAT leaflet "Transfer of a Business as a Going Concern".

Existing Staff Look carefully at the terms, conditions and rates of pay for existing staff as you have to observe these. Are the wages paid realistic? If you plan to reduce the number of staff you could be liable for redundancy payments. See the **Employing Staff** chapter.

Market Research One great advantage of buying over an existing business is that the need for doing a full market research is diminished (but not eliminated) because you have access to real trading figures gleaned from the accounts of the business. However, trading conditions vary constantly and you must do some market research to ensure that market conditions are not likely to vary adversely for the foreseeable future.

Premises Most businesses operate from an office, shop or factory. If you are contemplating taking over a business it is therefore imperative to enquire fully into the situation regarding the premises. Are the premises owned by the company or rented? If they are rented then how long is the lease for, are there restrictions on the use of the premises, how much is the rent, when is there a rent review and does the landlord have to approve any new tenant? Check the lease carefully. It is essential for a structural survey to be done and for you to find out if you would be responsible for the repairs and insurance of the building. The surveyor can also comment on the lease prior to you consulting your solicitor. See the chapter **Finding Premises**.

BUYING AN EXISTING BUSINESS YOUR NEXT STEPS –

If you are considering buying an existing business, after having read this section, you should:

1. Get the facts – details of stock, fixtures & fittings, machinery & equipment and staff; what value the owners place on the business; up-to-date accounts for the last 3 or 5 years; copy of lease (if premises are rented).

2. Do the necessary Market Research as described in the next chapter.

3. Prepare a Business Plan and raise the finance as described later.

4. Get good professional advice.

5. Do not sign anything until the above steps have been completed and, just like buying a second-hand car, do not be hurried into a decision by the seller saying others are interested or that he must have a reply within a few days.

KEY POINT — **There Are Many Ways To Make £££** There are many ways to make a living, but the lifestyle can vary enormously and this should be taken into account at this stage before you are saddled with debt, leases, stock, staff and so on. For instance, if you choose to open a small general store/newsagent, then you can expect to work a 7-day week with a very early start to the day. Shops in general have large stock, onerous leases (if rented) and often have continual staffing problems. But at least it is a cash business, ie your customers do not expect any credit. In contrast, many manufacturing concerns suffer from customers who take many months to pay (or never do!) and they usually have to operate on small margins – but at least they can close the door and go home on a Friday evening (even if they still take some of their paperwork home with them).

Some service businesses have the advantage of requiring little stock and have low overheads, but are frequently the type of business that is copied readily by competitors (or it may be the type of business where your customers expect you to answer the phone when they have a problem even at 9pm in the evening!).

These lifestyle aspects do need full consideration as they will be with you for the lifetime of your business■

BEFORE STARTING

Chapters

Doing the Market Research

This chapter is to help you answer the fundamental question: "Is there a market for my product (or service) and is it big enough to support me and my business?"

Finding the answer requires what is called "market research". If you start a business, almost any business, you will always be able to make some sales but what you really need to find out is will you be able to sell enough to make even a modest living? Frequently would-be entrepreneurs say "I'm not trying to make a lot of money, just enough to live on". But what they may not realise is that just to make enough money to survive might require more sales and success than they had anticipated. Here is a specific example ...

Assume you want to manufacture a car accessory which you plan to sell through car accessory shops. This particular product, called a SAYIT, attaches to the rear of a vehicle and when the driver wants to flash a message to the vehicle behind he merely operates a switch on the dashboard and the SAYIT lights up the word "Thanks" or "Sorry" as appropriate (or maybe something a little stronger!). The material cost in the device is approximately £5 and if it is wholesaled to the car accessory shops for £6 then the gross profit per unit will be £1. How many units do you think you need to sell to make the equivalent of a £6,000 wage? Is It 6000, 8000 or 10000?

It is not 6000 as you might suppose as you have other costs, called "overheads" to pay for, such as workshop rent/rates, telephone calls, postage, travel etc which may add up to £4,000 per year (or more). So to make £6,000 per year you will have to make and sell 10000 SAYITs. The question your market research must answer is "Will the market buy 10000 SAYITs per year at a wholesale price of £6?" Note that if 10000 SAYITs are likely to swamp the market then you will do little trade in your second year!

Market research can be thought of in 3 parts:

1. **Analysis of the market.**
2. **Analysis of competitors.**
3. **Testing the market** (before you fully commit yourself).

ANALYSIS OF THE MARKET

This gives you an inside picture of the trade you are thinking of entering, the trends both nationally and locally and an understanding of the needs of your potential customers. It is achieved as follows ...

The National Situation Many industries are described fully in market research studies carried out by organisations such as Mintel and Key Note and copies of their reports are available at large public libraries. You might also notice articles in newspapers or on television which refer to trends. Beware though of the "Media Bubble", where excessive coverage is given in the press and on TV to a new craze or trend. If one is to believe the media there appears to be a huge market and often dozens of firms will pop up in response but it is unlikely that the actual market size is large enough, or that the demand (if it existed in the first place) will be sustained.

Even if your proposed business does not need a national-sized market to sustain it, national trends can have a significant effect at a local level. You need to know if the industry you are entering is expanding, contracting, stable or very dependent upon another industry which itself is changing rapidly. There may even be legislation in the pipeline that could have a major effect on your plans.

Knowing trends has another significance, because those people who get on to the "band-wagon" of a new product or service early on often do much better than those who come along later, but of course the early entrepreneurs are exposed to greater risk. Good examples here are laundrettes and video hire shops, where the first people into the new market did very well indeed.

Two other good sources of information are trade magazines and trade shows. Ask your local librarian about the magazines and for details of trade shows ask your Enterprise Agency or get a copy of the publication "The Exhibition Bulletin" – a single copy costs £10 from tel: 081-778 2288.

The Local Situation Once you have some knowledge of the national situation and relevant trends you need to know much more about the trade on a more local level. To this end there is no better source of information than the trade itself! First of all speak to the sales representatives of your likely suppliers – they can provide good information if asked the correct questions. They are, after all, trying to engage your interest in their products so they should talk, reminisce and tell you their business problems if gently encouraged. This will build you up an interesting picture.

Next, through the assistance of your local Enterprise Agency or business development unit try to meet someone doing the same business in a different

Doing the Market Research

part of the town or county (so that you would not be in direct competition). You will be surprised how helpful most people can be.

KEY POINT Before you meet anyone, always write down the questions to ask. Take a note of their answers.

The Target Market This is the phrase used to describe that section of the population that could potentially use your product or service and is therefore your "target". For your business to succeed you need customers (that's obvious isn't it?) but have you stopped to think just who those people are and what exactly their needs are and what benefit they will get from using your product or service? They are obviously surviving without you at present so why will they want to use your business? Also, are there enough potential customers within reach of your business?

Before proceeding further you need to be clear as to whether you will be selling to trade customers, the general public or both. There are major differences between the two, for instance trade customers generally have larger budgets and different requirements, such as the design of the packaging, when goods are to be delivered or the date by which work must be completed. Another major difference is that trade customers expect credit – at least 30 days, sometimes much more, whereas a private customer is prepared to pay immediately.

This whole matter of credit can have fundamental implications for a new business as providing credit (or receiving credit from trade suppliers) can have a marked effect on your cashflow, and

giving credit costs you money and can lead to bad debts. Cashflows are discussed in a later chapter.

Trade Customers To do the market research, first prepare a list of all the companies who you believe may be interested in your product or service. Get their names from the Yellow Pages or a Trade Directory. You then need to contact them to find out their views on what you have to offer. Before you make such an approach you will need to know what your prices will be (see chapter **Marketing And Sales**). The technique then is to get an appointment, either by phoning first or writing a letter (see the example on page 73).

Private Customers If you are selling to the general public, trying to find out who will buy what from you is much more difficult than with trade customers. In this case try to start by asking people already in the trade as their customers are likely to be similar to yours. The next step is to speak directly to likely customers and the most thorough way of doing that with the general public is to use a questionnaire – see the end of this chapter.

KEY POINT There is no substitute for actually talking to your potential buyers and it is best done before you are committed to the project.

ANALYSIS OF COMPETITORS

A great deal of interesting and useful information can be derived from close observation of potential competitors. To locate competitors:

1. Consult the Yellow Pages and any Trade/Business Directory.

2. If your intended business is retail – walk the streets in the area where you are thinking of setting up and mark on a street plan the name and location of competitors.

3. Ask your suppliers' sales reps who else they supply in your area.

Checking-out the Competition
A number of techniques are possible:

1. Sit outside your competitors' premises (sit in a nearby café or in a car) and observe the people or vehicles

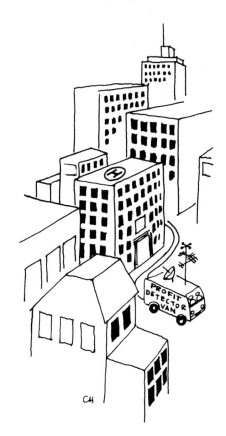

A number of techniques are possible....

coming and going. Take notes. This can reveal: In the case of shops – how many people go in and how many come out with purchases. In the case of factories – the names of suppliers/ customers (conveniently written on the sides of lorries/vans) and the general level of activity of the business, ie quiet or busy. In all cases this observation needs to be done at several different times of the day or week and for an hour or more at a time.

2.   If the competitor is a limited company, they have to file annual accounts and annual returns which are available to the general public for a small fee. They give the names of Directors and various financial details. For companies registered in England or Wales these details are available either by visiting: Companies House, 55-71 City Road, London EC1Y 1BB, tel: 071-253 9393 or by post from: Companies House, Crown Way, Maindy, Cardiff CF4 3UZ. Tel: Cardiff (0222) 388588.

For companies registered in Scotland, these details are available by post, by phone or by visiting: Companies House, 100-102 George Street, Edinburgh EH2 3DJ. Tel: 031-225 5774.

There are also Satellite Offices in Manchester, Birmingham, Leeds and Glasgow.

For companies registered in Northern Ireland, these details are available from: Companies Registry, IDB House, 64 Chichester Street, Belfast BT1 4JX. Tel: Belfast (0232) 234488.

3.   If the competitor is a manufacturer, try to buy, rent or borrow a sample of their product and check it out noting strengths and weaknesses. How does it compare with your own product? Note too any patent markings.

4.   If the competitor is in the service sector try to use their service or if that is not possible ask friends to phone as if they were customers and get them to ask about prices and how soon they can get the service (as this may reveal how busy your competitors are). This same technique could be used for manufacturers if data on their products is hard to acquire.

5.   Obtain pamphlets, sales literature and price lists whenever available, by writing, phoning or at trade shows where the competitor has a stand.

6.   If possible, try to speak to past or present customers – this can often be most revealing.

KEY POINT Keep a file on each competitor enclosing all the information you have built up on them.

Assessing The Situation Once you have completed the above market research (which may take several weeks or much longer), you will need to sit back and assess the situation. In particular you should by this stage be able to estimate if your proposed business venture will either increase the likely size of the market (most common with new products or services) or will it succeed only at the expense of your competitors? Sometimes it is a mixture of both, but the implications can be significant.

If you think you will be expanding the market it means new customers will be using you – where will they be coming from and what is it that attracts them? Are you expecting them to stop buying something to have the spare money to spend it with you?

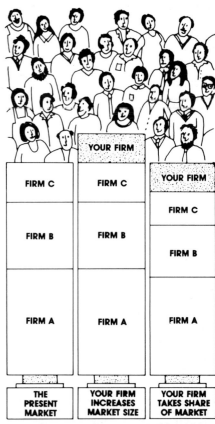

MARKET SHARE

Alternatively if you are trying to "muscle into" an existing market how will you win over customers from other suppliers? One way is to offer a better quality product or service. But when you start trading, there is a serious danger of counter-attack from existing businesses as they will not simply open the door to you. In contrast they are more likely to slam the door in your face. Such door-slamming techniques could include dropping their prices to

Doing the Market Research

engage you in a price war, poaching your key staff by offering higher wages or interfering with your sources of supply. In any event you would be unlikely to win unless you have enormous resources behind you, so it is worth thinking about and should never be underestimated.

TESTING THE MARKET

This is not always necessary but it can be very useful where the other market research carried out is rather inconclusive. Test marketing is sometimes called "flying a kite" or "putting a toe in the water" and that helps to explain what it is about. Its function is simply to test the market reaction to a new product or service with the minimum of investment and is usually done at an early stage before one is fully committed to the project. It is a very common practice and takes a number of forms:

The Advert   This is the simplest way to check the market though it has limitations (see chapter **Marketing and Sales**). With this form of test marketing you advertise a product or service as if it were actually available (even if you are not quite at that stage) to see what reaction it produces. But note your advert must not be misleading.

The Sample   If it is a product you are making which is to be sold to the trade you take samples to potential customers and take orders before committing yourself to full production. This practice is common in the fashion and gift trades.

The Mailshot   In this case you send a letter to any potential customer requesting a response which would indicate their interest in what you have to offer. This can be a very effective technique especially if the customers are businesses and the letters are addressed to named individuals or appropriate posts (see the example on page 73).

The Leaflet Drop   A version of the mailshot but less personal and best suited for the general public by slipping the leaflets through their letter boxes. It can also be used for trade customers or could be inserted into newspapers or magazines (called "inserts").

The Exhibition/Trade Show   Yet another way to judge market reaction to your product or service is to rent a stand at a suitable exhibition or trade show. It is useful because unlike all the above options (except **The Sample**) you get immediate feedback from potential customers. This can be crucial in helping you to fine tune your product or service, establish prices etc. Note that participating in exhibitions can be very costly in terms of cash and time. Also, the success of them should be judged on the contacts made and not necessarily the amount of business done on site.

In Conclusion   In most test marketing an element of bluff is essential, particularly if you have not yet commenced trading and are trying out the market before you commit yourself. Since nobody particularly wants to deal with a "business" that is just starting or operating from a garden shed (or worse!), the use of first, a business name and second, a trade address could be beneficial though not essential. Trading under a business name is easy (see chapter **Making it Legal**) but finding a trade address could present more of a problem.

AND FINALLY ...

The market research you will have to do forms a fundamental part of the Business Plan which comes after the next chapter in this book. Many people think that market research is only done before starting a business or launching a new product or service. In fact

---

10 Common Errors When Doing Market Research

1. Speaking to everyone except the actual potential buyers.
2. Failing to notice warning signals as you are convinced your project will work.
3. Asking "loaded" questions, the answers to which just confirm your ideas without revealing the interviewee's thoughts.
4. Ignoring the fact that often 20% of the customers provide 80% of the turnover.
5. Assuming you will compete effectively just because your prices will be lower.
6. Being influenced by your contacts who promise to supply you with lots of work when you start. (Ask yourself how they are getting by without you now, and ask your contacts for more details of their needs to test their genuineness).
7. Underestimating how long it can take to enter a market and take a reasonable market share (it's years, not months).
8. Failing to recognise the strength and the reaction of the competition.
9. Basing your likely sales estimates on the simple assumption that you will take x% of the total market.
10. Forgetting that new products or ideas take time and money to introduce to the market. (People are very conservative).

market research should be thought of as an on-going activity and is covered further in the later chapter **Marketing and Sales**. When you start trading remember to follow up the sales leads and potential jobs you found when doing the market research.

QUESTIONNAIRES

The first way to get an idea of people's needs in a general sense is to read market research reports (as mentioned earlier). However, those are usually researched on a national scale. To find out more about the needs, views and habits of local consumers, you need to ask them and this is best done using a questionnaire. The 5 golden rules of questionnaires are:

* Keep it short and simple.

* Do not "load" the questions.

* Do not ask "open" questions.

* Ask likely customers.

* Ask as many people as you can.

Keeping It Short And Simple Ask yourself, what is it you are trying to find out. Ask only the most important questions and avoid any fringe issues. There should be no more than 5 to 10 questions. A multiple choice or Yes/No format is best as it is both easier to answer and quicker to analyse.

"Loaded" Questions If you were considering buying a mobile shop then you might ask householders in the appropriate district as to their views to assess if the business would be viable. A question such as "Do you buy anything from a mobile shop at present?" would be a reasonable question but if you were to ask "Would you use a mobile shop if it was cheaper?" invites

Do not ask "open" questions.

the answer "yes" without much consideration as it is a "loaded" question. In this case it may be more useful to ask the householders what time of day they were at home so you could plan your round. It is very easy to fall into the trap of asking "loaded" questions. Try to avoid emotive or exaggerated phrases in the question. Also, be aware that people often naturally give the reply which they think you want to hear.

"Open" Questions The purpose of the questionnaire is to find out precise answers to specific questions so you

can draw conclusions. The danger of "open" questions such as "Do you think mobile shops are a good idea?" is that it could lead to a long debate! Instead, to each question on the questionnaire the answer should be either yes/no or one answer of a multiple choice. In general, avoid asking for people's opinions, stick to the facts. (As your experience increases, you can try a more open question as sometimes they can be most revealing).

Ask The Right People To get the right people might involve house-to-house interviews or if doing the survey in the main street stop only those people who you think might use your product or service. There may be places that your likely customers congregate. For instance if you were planning to set up a business selling sports equipment obviously you would visit local gyms, local athletics clubs etc. Remember you do not need the name of the person you are interviewing.

Ask Many People Within reason the more people you ask the more accurate will be your survey. To make the analysis of the survey data easier you could type out one questionnaire and photocopy it so that with each person you ask, you complete a new sheet. This makes adding up the figures at the end easier. You should ask at least 100 people, maybe many more if possible■

Making it Legal

Once you have completed your market research the next step is to prepare a Business Plan but before you can do that it is necessary to digress briefly to look at the essential legalities to consider when starting a business. Note this chapter excludes the legal aspects associated with premises as this is covered in the **Finding Premises** chapter while patents and similar legal protection of "intellectual property" are covered in the chapter **Thinking of a Business Idea**. It is important to speak to a solicitor at an early stage.

Sole Trader/Partnership/Limited Company or Co-operative? An early decision is what legal form the business should take. If you are going to be a one-boss business you could be a "sole trader" (ie self-employed) or a "limited company" while if there is going to be several "bosses" you need to be a "partnership", "limited company" or "co-operative". Some people think that they must form a limited company when they start in business but this is not necessarily the case.

Sole Trader This is probably the most common form when a business starts. You can trade under your own name or a business name (see below). You can also employ staff. Should the business fail owing money, then your creditors can seize your personal possessions to recover their losses. Many businesses start as "sole trader" but as they grow they usually change to a "limited company" status for two reasons: a) the limited liability protection of their personal possessions and b) it is easier for them to raise larger sums of money for expansion.

Partnership If two or more people work together and no-one is an "employee" then the law regards the arrangement as a "partnership", which has important consequences. Most importantly, each partner will be "jointly and severally liable" for any debts the business runs up. What this means in practice is if Partner A buys a car using a business cheque which subsequently bounces, the car dealer can pursue Partner B for the entire amount! Also, unless there is an agreement to the contrary, profits in a partnership have to be shared equally between partners.

It is a sad truth that many partners come to blows but this could be avoided if the partners started off with a good written Partnership Agreement.

It is a sad truth that many partners come to blows.

See the example at the end of the chapter – roughly draft your own agreement based on this and then see a solicitor and an accountant. There are many complex issues involved and you will need proper advice. You may not need all the clauses listed in the example or you may even like to add new clauses.

If, due to personal circumstances, the partners contribute different amounts of capital then they can choose to either: a) apportion the profits in the same ratio as the amounts invested or b) allow time, say 6 months, for the partners to equalise their investments to allow the profits to be shared equally. In both cases voting rights should be equal as well as personal drawings.

Choose your partner(s) carefully. They could lead to your personal bankruptcy just as easily as helping you to make a profit. It may be better for them to be employees rather than partners. Finally, remember to take out "cross insurance" which is a life assurance policy payable to the other partner(s) in the event of a partner dying to enable the surviving partner(s) to purchase the deceased partner's share of the business from his estate and to continue trading.

Limited Company Unlike a sole trader a limited liability company is a legal entity in its own right. Its shareholders and Directors may change but the company will continue to exist until wound up. Companies have many laws to regulate them and no-one should consider setting up a company without fully understanding the implications and having taken professional advice. A limited company used to require a minimum of two shareholders (who

Making it Legal

could be husband and wife) but since 1992, Single Member Companies have been permitted. A company must have at least one Director. The company must also have a company secretary who could be a second Director, another shareholder or your accountant or solicitor.

Companies House (addresses on page 17) produce a series of free small booklets which give more advice and are highly recommended reading.

Directors derive benefits by being paid an employee's salary or fees while shareholders get paid "dividends" out of the profits. One can buy an "off-the-shelf" company for around £150-£200 and this can be done within days. Only buy from a reputable company to ensure what you are buying is indeed a "clean" company without liabilities. Contact your solicitor or look under "Company Registration Agents" in the Yellow Pages. Winding up a company,

You can buy an "off the shelf" company.

in contrast, can be much more expensive and protracted.

Co-operative A co-operative can be thought of as a specialised form of limited company. Here we are referring to "workers' co-operatives" rather than the high street shop groups that also use this name. Co-operatives are run like any other small business with managers or supervisors, the difference being that the business is owned by everyone who works in it and any decisions are made democratically.

Workers' co-operatives are still quite rare in the United Kingdom. Get further information from ICOM (the Industrial Common Ownership Movement) at Vassalli House, 20 Central Road, Leeds LS1 6DE, tel: 0532 461738. In Scotland, contact the Scottish Co-operative Development Company (tel: 041-554 3797) and in Wales, the Wales Co-operative Development and Training Centre (tel: 0222 554955).

Business Names

A sole trader can trade under his own name (married name if a woman) ie as William Smith, W. Smith, Wm. Smith, Smith or William David Smith and a partnership can trade under the names of all the partners. But if a business name is to be used (eg "Smith's Giftshop") then the requirements of the Business Names Act 1985 apply. The Act prevents you from using certain words in a business name and regulates the disclosure of business ownership (as detailed below).

Sensitive Words You cannot use any name for your business – it must not be offensive and the use of certain words needs approval, eg Limited (unless you are incorporated), International, National, British, Scottish, Irish, English, Welsh, European, Royal, Group, Trust, Society, Breeder, Registered etc. A list of such words and how you might get permission to use them is given in the booklets "Business Names and Business Ownership" and "Sensitive Words And Expressions" available from any Companies House.

Note that as there is no registration of business names, someone else might unintentionally use the same name unless you formed a limited company (as no two companies can have exactly the same name).

Limited Liability Company or Sole Trader/Partnership?

Advantages of Ltd Co: Limited liability of Directors and shareholders (ie should the company fail, in most cases all you would lose is your share capital); easier to raise larger sums of money; easier format to cope with investors who do not want to work in the business.

Disadvantages of Ltd Co: Directors' wages subject to PAYE; higher annual accountancy charges; overall taxation sometimes greater due to high National Insurance contributions; public disclosure of some key data; cannot offset losses against your previous income tax.

Making it Legal

Disclosure of Ownership The Business Names Act also requires:

1. Business Stationery All letterheads, orders, invoices, receipts, statements and demands must carry in addition to the business name, the names of all the owners and in relation to each person named an address "at which documents can be served" (normally the business address). Refer also to the letterheads illustrated on page 62.

2. Business Premises Sign This same information must be displayed prominently and legibly on a sign in all the places where you carry on your business and deal with customers or suppliers. There are no set rules as to the design of this sign but one suggestion is illustrated below. Note that the size of the sign should be commensurate with its surroundings.

3. On Request The names and addresses of all owners of the business has to be given immediately in writing when requested by any supplier, customer or other person with whom the business has dealings.

Companies: The Business Names Act also applies to any company that uses a trading name other than its own, eg if "ABC Foods (XYZ) Ltd" wishes to trade simply as "ABC Foods".

In addition, the Companies Act requires a company to paint or affix its name on the *outside* of every office or place where it carries on business.

See also the free Companies House booklet "Choosing a Company Name".

Note there are special rules for Welsh companies.

Licences/Registration You can start most businesses right away as there is no need for registration or licensing, but there are exceptions, examples being: selling liquor; providing driving instruction; operating an employment agency; dealing with scrap metal; providing public entertainment; dealing in second-hand goods; operating as a street trader or mobile shop; driving a taxi or private hire car; operating certain goods and passenger vehicles; cleaning windows; hair-dressing; selling door-to-door; most activities relating to pets or animals and providing credit services (see "Consumer Credit Act" below). Also, if you are going to sell or handle food you must speak to the Environmental Health Department at a very early stage of the project (and before you start trading).

The list above is only a sample and failure to obtain a licence may be a criminal offence.

KEY POINT Contact your Enterprise Agency or local Council to ascertain if your project requires a licence or other approval.

PARTICULARS OF OWNERSHIP
of

SIMPLY PERFECT

as required by the Business Names Act 1985

Full Name(s) of Owner(s)	Address at which Documents can be served
Miss Joan Smith	12, Regent Crescent Greenock PA1 1ZZ

An example of a sign, completed with fictitious particulars

Consumer Credit Act In most cases if you are going to provide credit, arrange credit or HP or if you are going to hire equipment for more than 3 months, then you are likely to need a licence under this Act.

You may not need a licence if, for instance, you are simply accepting payment by credit card or you are simply allowing customers to pay their bills at the end of the week, month or whatever period you work to (this includes normal "trade" credit).

The Act is complex and it is a criminal offence to give credit without a licence unless the exceptions such as mentioned above apply. So if you are in any doubt, it is essential you contact your local Trading Standards Department without delay.

Data Protection Act If you are going to keep information about people on a computer, even if it is just names and addresses, then you need to become registered (costs currently £75). For a form and further information contact the Registrar's Enquiry Service on tel: Wilmslow (0625) 535777.

Financial Services Act This Act requires anyone involved in the provision of financial advice, or related services, to register.

Food Safety Act & other Regulations There are stringent rules regarding most aspects of handling, preparing and selling food. For instance, equipment, premises, food handlers, storage, working methods, labelling etc are all covered. Speak to your local Environmental Health Department at the very start of your project.

Insurance It is a legal requirement to have vehicle insurance and Employers Liability Insurance (and certain Engineering insurances). You should also be adequately insured for other risks. You should therefore discuss your proposed venture with an insurance broker (who should be registered and a member of the British Insurance and Investment Brokers Association).

The broker may only be able to give you an estimate at this early stage as you probably will not have the full details they require. The various types of insurance which you may consider are covered below.

Note: The Association of British Insurers (Tel: 071-600 3333) produce a useful £1 booklet which gives insurance advice for small businesses.

Employers Liability A legal requirement only if you employ someone and the certificate has to be prominently displayed at the place of work. This insurance is to protect employers against claims for damages, brought by employees for death or bodily injury sustained in the course of employment (which includes injury caused by other employees for whom you are liable). It is not required by sole-traders or partnerships with no employees.

Public Liability This provides you with protection against claims for which you may be legally liable brought by anyone other than employees for bodily injury or loss or damage to property arising in the course of your business. It also covers the legal costs defending such claims.

Product Liability This provides protection for legal liability for claims arising from injury, loss or damage due to products you have sold, supplied, repaired, serviced or tested.

Professional Indemnity This is for anyone starting a business as a consultant (legal, management, technical, marketing, financial etc). This protects you against your legal liability to compensate third parties who have sustained some injury, loss or damage due to your own professional negligence or that of your employees.

Vehicles If you intend to use your car or van in the business, check that your insurance covers you (and any other driver) for the commercial purpose you propose. Generally for a car there will be an additional premium for using it in connection with your business.

Goods In Transit As a rule motor insurance policies do not cover goods being carried in the vehicle so if you intend to carry goods you may need this additional insurance cover.

Premises If you are buying premises or it is a condition of the lease that you should insure the premises, then you should be covered against fire and special perils (eg burst pipes, storms, malicious damage). Check too that your plate glass windows (where relevant) are covered. Your insurance broker will advise you if it is necessary to be covered for "Property Owners Liability" as this risk may already be covered by the Public Liability policy.

Stock, Fixtures & Fittings, Plant and Machinery Be careful not to underestimate the value of these. Note that if your cover is for "reinstatement value" it provides for the full replacement cost while "indemnity value" is the current market value less depreciation (which can be significant!). Insurance should cover losses due to theft, vandalism, fire, flood etc. Accidental damage or "all risks" cover can also be arranged in many cases if so required.

Making it Legal

Engineering If the business has plant or machinery which must have a periodic statutory inspection then it is usual to arrange for this to be done by a specialist engineering insurer under an inspection contract, with or without insurance cover on the plant or machinery.

Money If your business involves handling cash in significant amounts then insurance cover against theft would be prudent. Policies normally cover loss of money in the premises and also money in transit to or from the bank. If covered for cash in transit be sure to comply with the small print.

Once the business is established you may also want to consider:

Employment Protection When you are employing people, particularly if it is a large number, the complex employment legislation which covers employees rights, unfair dismissal, redundancies and so on can cripple a small company both financially and in management time when things start to go wrong. This insurance covers not only legal fees but can also cover personnel advisory services that you will need.

Fidelity Guarantee & Internal Theft This provides protection against dishonesty or theft by members of your own staff.

Consequential Loss If your office, shop or factory is put out of commission due to fire or any other insured peril then this insurance will maintain the financial position of the company as if the calamity had not occurred. Such insurance can be expensive but failure to have it can in certain circumstances close a business down permanently when such a disaster occurs.

Personal Health/Life and Pensions It is wise to consider Personal Health Insurance cover for yourself to provide you with an income should you be unable to work. This is a very important matter and should not be overlooked. Similarly, if the company is very dependent upon one or two key people it may be wise to insure these people against death, accident or sickness for the business may suffer financially in the event of their death or prolonged absence from work. As the company's fortunes increase you should also consider life assurance and pensions for yourself and perhaps for your staff.

Finally, remember that the services of an insurance broker are free as he is paid commission by the insurance companies. A good broker will not try to sell you insurance you do not require but at the same time he will be concerned that you do not under-insure. It is a balancing act to a certain extent as you should take out as much insurance as you need, but no more and no less — and in any event you must review the position at least once a year to take into account changes in your business.

Inland Revenue (Tax, PAYE) As a sole trader or partner you do not pay PAYE (Pay-As-You-Earn) income tax which all employees have to pay. Instead you pay your income tax on the profits of the business after it is calculated by your accountant at the end of the tax year. You do not get the first year free of tax — you simply have to pay it all later! You should therefore save some of your takings to allow you to pay your tax liability.

KEY POINT When you start trading you must notify the Inspector of Taxes.

Unless you are going to incorporate a limited company this notification is done on a Form 41G which is available from your local Inland Revenue office. See opposite. (A limited company makes a similar notification to the Inland Revenue on a Form CT41G).

If you are employing people you have to operate PAYE. Remember that if you are a limited company, you must also operate PAYE for Directors. Contact your local PAYE office (look under "Inland Revenue" in the Phone Book) and ask for a "New Employer's Starter Pack" — it is heavy going, so see also the chapter **Coping with Taxation** later in this book.

National Insurance As a sole trader or partner you will normally each have to pay a regular Class 2 contribution and your business will in addition have to pay a Class 4 contribution if your profits exceed a certain figure. If your self-employed earnings are likely to be small, you can apply for a Small Earnings Exception. (Refer to the **Tax Data Page** at the end of this book).

KEY POINT When you start trading as a sole trader or partnership you must notify the DSS.

Visit your local Social Security office (Benefits Agency) and ask for the appropriate leaflets for a self-employed person. You can elect to pay your Class 2 contributions monthly direct from your business bank account. You should not complete this direct debit mandate until you have actually started your business, ie when you are committed.

24

Enquiries about the business	Replies

1. In what name is the business carried on, if not in your own name?

1. _____

2. What is the business address, including postcode, if different from your private address?

2. **SPECIMEN**

_____ Postcode _____

3. What is the nature of the business?

3. _____

4. When did you start in this business?

4. 10

5. If you took over an existing business, who did you acquire it from?

5.
Name _____
Address _____
_____
_____ Postcode _____

6. To what date do you propose to make up your business accounts?

If they are to be prepared by a firm of accountants, please give their name and address including postcode.

6. 19

Name _____
Address _____
_____
_____ Postcode _____

7. If you are not already operating PAYE as an employer, have you any employees earning
   - more than £53.50 a week or £232 a month?
   - more than £1 a week who have other employment?

7.
Yes No
☐ ☐
☐ ☐   *Please '✓' appropriate box.*

Personal enquiries	Replies

8. Were you employed or were you self employed before you started this business?

What was the name and address of the business or employer. Please give this information even if you had a period of unemployment between leaving employment and starting your own business.

If you still have the leaving certificate form P45 handed to you by your last employer, please attach it and give the leaving date.

8. Employed ☐   Self employed ☐   *'✓' one box*

Name _____
Address _____
_____
_____ Postcode _____

19

9. If this is your first occupation since leaving full time education on what date did the education finish?

9. 19

10. If as well as running your business you are in paid employment, or are continuing an existing business, please give the name and address of the employer/existing business.

10.
Name _____
Address _____
_____
_____ Postcode _____

Is this an existing business or employment?

Existing business ☐   Employment ☐   *'✓' one box*

Signature _____   Date   19

Please say whether you are single, married, widowed, separated or divorced _____

Making it Legal

This visit would also permit you to discuss how your proposed business will affect any social security benefits that you may be in receipt of.

If you form a limited company, as a Director you need to pay Class 1 contributions. In addition the company has to pay an "employer's contribution". These are both payable to the Inland Revenue with your PAYE. The procedure is shown on pages 108 & 109.

Customs & Excise (VAT) Value Added Tax is a tax on most business transactions, including importing goods and some imported services. With few exceptions you will need to register for VAT if, at the end of any month, the total value of the "taxable supplies" you have made in the past 12 months exceeds the VAT registration threshold. For the current threshold figure, see the **Tax Data Page** at the end of this book. If you exceed the threshold prior to completing your first 12 months in business, then you need to register immediately. Registration is also required if at any time there are reasonable grounds for believing that the value of the taxable supplies you will make in the next 30 days will exceed the threshold.

"Taxable supplies" are all your sales (other than those that are "exempt supplies", as described below).

For VAT purposes, all business transactions come under one of three categories:

Exempt Supplies This applies to only those very few types of business which are specified as "exempt" from VAT, such as insurance. No VAT is payable and you cannot be VAT registered if you only make exempt supplies.

Zero Rated This applies to only those types of business which are specified as "zero-rated" for VAT. There are more examples than for exempt businesses, including: young children's clothing and footwear, books, newspapers, public transport and basic foodstuffs (but not catering). No VAT is payable. If your turnover exceeds the threshold then you need to register in which case you can recover any VAT on business expenses but there is no need to add VAT to your sales (as they are zero-rated). You could instead choose to apply for exemption from registration if your taxable supplies are mainly or wholly zero-rated.

Standard Rated This rate applies to almost all other business transactions!

If your business falls into this category and your turnover has exceeded the VAT threshold you must register for VAT. You must then add VAT to your prices but you can recover the VAT you are charged.

To register for VAT, contact your local Customs & Excise Office. See under "Customs & Excise" in the Phone Book. Refer also to the chapter **Coping with Taxation**.

VAT is a complex tax, but the free VAT booklet "Should I Be Registered for VAT?" is easy to read and essential reading for any business. It also includes a VAT Registration Application Form and notes how to complete it.

General Many trades and industries have regulations that apply specifically to them. You should ask the appropriate trade association for more information.

NOTE Please note this chapter is for general guidance only and should not be regarded as a complete or authoritative statement of the law. For more information, please contact the relevant authorities.

PARTNERSHIP AGREEMENT

(Note: This is a fictitious example to show you what a Partnership Agreement might look like. The details are of course relevant only to this specific example. Your own agreement should be produced by your solicitor and reflect your own particular circumstances).

We, the undersigned, herein after known as Tring-A-Ling Alarms, and intending to work together in business, agree to the following terms of Partnership:

1. Nature of Business.   The business will be the supply, installation and maintenance of security equipment, and such other business as may be agreed by all the partners.

2. Location of Business.   The business will be located at 10 Sellers Lane, London EC1, and at such other place or places as may be agreed by all the partners.

3. Date of Commencement[1]   The partnership will commence on 1st May 1990 with the partners sharing equal responsibility and liability.

4. Initial Capital.   Each partner undertakes to provide at the date of commencement the sum of £5,000 (Five Thousand Pounds). They further agree not to remove the said sum without the consent of all partners.

5. Role of Partners[2]   All partners undertake to work full time and give their best endeavours to the furtherance of the business. The partners will not undertake other paid or unpaid employment or self-employment or be associated with any other business during the period of this Agreement. No partner without the consent of the other partner(s) shall enter into or terminate any contract for the purchase of goods or services exceeding £1,000, offer employment to any person or terminate the employment of any staff, nor enter into or terminate any property lease arrangements, nor lend any property or assets of the business[3].

6. Voting Rights & Arbitration.   All decisions pertaining to the business will require the approval of all partners. In the event of disagreement, arbitration will be undertaken by the firm's appointed accountant[4].

7. Bank Account.   A bank account in the name of the business is to be opened at the Anytown Branch of the XYZ Bank plc. Thereafter any partner can draw cheques for routine business expenditure up to a maximum of £100. Cheques drawn for amounts in excess of that figure require the signature of two partners. All other documents require the signature of all partners. All cheques and monies received on account of the business are to be paid into the partnership account on receipt.

8. Profits & Losses.   Profits and losses will be divided equally. The partnership will appoint a qualified Chartered Accountant who will prepare the business accounts annually within 60 days of the end of the Tax Year. Goodwill is to be disregarded when

8. (cont'd) computing profits. The partnership books are normally to be kept at the place of business.

9. <u>Drawings & Expenses</u>.   The partners may each draw up to £120 per week. Should there be insufficient funds to meet these drawings, the amount will automatically reduce to that which the funds can meet. The amount is to be reviewed each January. Should any partner elect to leave his drawings in the business he shall be entitled to interest at the current Bank Base Rate and payable quarterly in arrears on the average amount left in the business bank account over that quarter. In addition each partner can draw expenses to cover expenditure on motor fuel but only if incurred in connection with the business and to a maximum of £1000 per annum[5].

10. <u>Holidays</u>.   After six months have elapsed, each partner may take up to three weeks paid annual holiday, the dates of which are to be agreed by all partners.

11. <u>Incapacity</u>.   If in the event of illness or accident a partner is unable to perform his duties his rights and benefits remain intact for three months. Thereafter the remaining partner(s) may elect to expel the incapacitated partner without further notice by sending a letter of intent, by recorded delivery, to his last known address.
The procedure for paying out the incapacitated partner is then (as given at Clause 13 below).

12. <u>Admission of New Partners</u>.   Before any new partner is admitted all partners must agree as to first, the capital the new partner should introduce to the business and second, what rights and benefits he or she should enjoy.

13. <u>Retirement[6] of Partners</u>.   A partner may retire from the partnership at any time by giving three months notice in writing sent to the business address. The retired partner's share shall pass to the continuing partner(s) on the date of retirement. The retiring partner is entitled to an equal share of the business assets, excluding goodwill[7], as valued by the firm's accountants by reference to a balance sheet made up to the date of retirement. This share is to be paid in cash to the retiring partner in four equal parts payable, without interest, on the following anniversaries of the date of retirement, namely three months, six months, nine months and twelve months.

14. <u>Dissolution of Partnership</u>[8]   The partnership may be dissolved by agreement of all the partners. In the event of dissolution, all equipment, stock and other assets owned by the partnership are to be sold and the proceeds divided equally after all debts have been settled to the satisfaction of the firm's accountants.

15. <u>Death</u>.   It is expressly agreed that in the event of death of a partner the partnership will continue. In the event of death of a partner during the currency of this Agreement then the deceased partner's share shall pass to the remaining partner(s) on the date of

15. (cont'd) such death. The estate of the deceased partner is entitled to a proportionate share of the business assets, excluding goodwill, as valued by the firm's accountants by reference to a balance sheet made up to the date of such death. This share is to be paid in cash to the deceased's estate in four equal parts payable, without interest, on the following anniversaries of the date of such death, namely one month, three months, six months and twelve months.

16. Income Tax. Each partner binds himself and his executors to sign if called upon to do so by the remaining partner(s), an election under the Income and Corporation Taxes Act 1988, or any re-enactment thereof, to have the profits of the business assessed to Income Tax on a continuation basis as if no change in the partnership had taken place.

17. Unfair Competition. (See Note No[9]).

Signatures of all Partners, Witnesses, Date and Place[10].

Author's Notes

(1) Some Agreements also state the duration for which the Agreement is to last, though such a clause would also usually allow the partners to extend the period.

(2) Where one partner is a "sleeping partner", this Clause would obviously need adjusting.

(3) It is difficult to guard against all reckless acts by individual partners which can create friction, but the items listed here are common problem areas.

(4) Alternatively you could refer to the local President of the Chamber of Commerce to nominate an arbitrator.

(5) With expenses it is wise to state an upper limit per annum. Other expenses such as business phone calls made from home may also be covered here.

(6) Many partnerships collapse when a partner chooses to leave demanding his share immediately. It is an important clause therefore and should embrace: a) an independent valuation of the business and b) payments phased over a period that is both fair to the outgoing partner and affordable by the remaining partners. The timescales for payments might be much longer than given in this example.

(7) In my opinion when a business is valued in this context,

"goodwill" should be excluded for the following reasons: a) any goodwill the business has built up has already been enjoyed by the outgoing partner by way of shared profits, b) the outgoing partner may have been the main factor behind any goodwill the business has built up and with his departure will reduce or disappear and c) it is a difficult aspect to quantify.

(8) A Partnership Agreement may also include a clause that allows the expulsion of one partner under certain specified circumstances.

(9) It is a good idea to incorporate an "Unfair Competition" clause in the Agreement if you are concerned that your partner(s) may leave the business at some time in the future and set up in competition with you. However, the wording of such a clause can be tricky and it cannot attempt to prevent a person from earning a livelihood.

(10) The witnesses are merely witnessing the signatures of the partners, they do not need to see the contents of the Agreement. It is better if they witness all partners signing. Note that Scots Law and English Law differ in respect of the requirements for signing and witnessing.

(General) If one or more of the partners are women then the provisions that apply to maternity leave and profit sharing during her absence ought to be included in the Agreement.

Preparing the Business Plan

One of the first steps in starting any new business should be the preparation of a Business Plan. What is a "Business Plan" you might ask? It is a planning document which sets out in both words and figures a proposed business venture. This can either be a new business start-up or a major expansion/diversification of an existing business. The need for a Business Plan is as relevant to the business that only requires £1,000 to set up as to the business that needs £1 million.

A Business Plan should be drafted by the people behind the venture with suitable advice and help from an accountant and possibly their local Enterprise Agency or business development unit. There is a worked example at the end of this chapter for the fictitious shop, which we have called "Simply Perfect".

The purposes of any Business Plan are to:

1. **Transfer your thoughts to paper.**
2. **Raise finance.**
3. **Monitor the project.**

These three points are now looked at in more detail...

Transferring Thoughts To Paper

When you are starting a business project there are many aspects to consider. Some are conflicting and others are easily influenced by perhaps a casual remark. By putting down the whole business idea in a structured, organised plan the situation is clarified and you can assess the project more objectively. Furthermore to complete the plan you have to answer a lot of questions and this forces you to go out and do the necessary "legwork" to find answers, which is in itself an excellent discipline.

Raising Finance

The Business Plan is the key to open the financier's coffers. A Business Plan is written in a language that is understood by financiers and bank managers and is laid out in the sort of format which they are used to. The document should be persuasive, conveying your enthusiasm for the project. Even if you are not planning to borrow money to get your business started, the preparation of a Business Plan could save you losing your own funds.

Monitoring The Project

The Business Plan lays down the path along which the business should be moving. When a business is started there are an enormous amount of things to do and in all the hurrying here and rushing there it is very easy to delude oneself that the business is doing well just because you are busy. With the Business Plan at your side, you can every so often, say monthly, take stock of the situation and check if you are still moving along the planned path (particularly in terms of the Cashflow Forecast). If not, remedial action can be taken and the sooner the better. Cashflow Management is discussed in more detail in the chapter **Controlling The Finances.**

FORMAT OF THE PLAN

A Business Plan can be laid out in a number of different formats though the information contained is similar. Here one particular format is suggested which is both clear and successful. At the end of the chapter is an example. Your own Business Plan may have longer or shorter sections than the example to tailor it to your own project.

*It's a marvelous business idea
Which simply cannot go wrong,
But the profits galore
Which we'll make, I'm sure,
Need a loan to help
them along!*

Avoid too many salesman's adjectives!

When writing the Business Plan try to avoid too many salesman's adjectives – so phrases such as ... "the wonderful new product..." or "this amazing service..." should be rationed to keep the plan convincing.

With the example you will notice there is a cover sheet, several pages of text (typed, never handwritten) followed by a Cashflow Forecast. The same model of Business Plan can be used for any business venture, with larger projects adding a Projected Balance Sheet.

For large scale projects the format is the same except there is usually more detail (ie the document is thicker!).

Preparing the Business Plan

In some cases the Business Plan needs supporting documentation which can be bound within the same covers or simply attached. For instance in projects where there is an involved technical process there could be significant data on the technical side, covering design, production matters and enclosing relevant drawings, charts and photos. You could also enclose sales literature if relevant.

In many larger projects an independent market research report would be required to give credibility to the plan and again this would be attached to the Business Plan and cross-referred to in the text.

GENERAL POINTS

The cover should give a professional look to the document. It gives the name(s) of the people behind the project, the business name and address of the business (or your home address if the business project does not yet have premises) and sometimes the name and address of your accountants if they have been closely involved in the preparation of the Business Plan. The whole document itself should be crisp, neat and free from speling erors!?

In terms of the text, it is usually written in the third person (eg "the proprietor" or, as in the case of the sample, "Miss Smith"). In contrast, existing businesses may use the first person plural, ie "we". In either case the text should be written with a reader in mind who has never met you and does not know anything about you, your business and maybe even your town — so spell out everything. The Business Plan should emphasise 4 key aspects which financial backers look for: evidence of *market research, planning, financial control* and the *competence* of the people behind the project.

HEADINGS

Summary   This is a summary of the relevant points of the following sheets which allows the reader to sum up the plan at a glance. The larger the plan the more useful is this section.

Contents   (This is only for Business Plans with more than, say, 10 pages). At this part of the Business Plan you would have a list of Contents together with the page number so the reader can locate a specific topic quickly. Our sample Business Plan omits a Contents as it is quite a short Plan.

Introduction   This is where you make a clear statement outlining the business project and its objectives. Usually one or two paragraphs suffice. If several phases are envisaged this should be mentioned. If a purpose of writing the Business Plan is to raise the necessary finance, this should be clearly stated.

Business History   This section is only completed where you are buying over an existing business or the Business Plan is by an existing company that is planning a major expansion/diversification.

In this section you would cover the following — the date the business started (usually date of incorporation if a limited company) and a note of any major recent events in the business's history. You would also state the main products or services, markets, and the particular strengths that have made the business successful.

In addition this section would have a statement on the company's present financial position and would refer to the latest accounts (which would be enclosed at the back of the Business Plan). For larger projects the last 3 years accounts may be required.

Personnel   *(Management)* This section gives the credentials of the proprietor(s) or Director(s) of the business — providing details of age, qualifications, personal means (eg property ownership), other business connections and most importantly, relevant experience.

In the case of a major project this section may need to refer to complete curricula vitae (enclosed at the back of the Business Plan).

If it is intended to recruit senior staff for the project, eg a Sales Manager, a statement would be made here to that effect.

For anyone embarking on his or her first business it is hoped they would attend a business course and in this section you could then make a comment to that effect. In addition if the proprietor(s) are receiving advice and support from an Enterprise Agency or other business development unit it is also useful to mention that here. All this is very important as financial backers are as concerned about the *people* they back as their *projects.*

(Staff) This section requires a statement on the staff you will need — how many, with what skills, likely wages you would have to pay, full-time or part-time and what training would be necessary. In some cases this section would indicate a phased increase as the business grows.

Product (or Service)   (whichever title is appropriate). This section

Preparing the Business Plan

describes in some detail the product or service your business will be offering.

For a product that is to be manufactured you need to mention its present state of development, ie initial design, prototype, pre-production or limited production stage. If it is an established product, how long it has been in production, how many have been made etc. A photograph or two, rather than a technical drawing, at the back of the report may greatly help the reader's understanding of the product.

In the case of a service business, in this section one would specify precisely what the service is and for what types of customers.

Market Research & Marketing Plan This is a most important section which in most cases should take at least a page of text and in larger projects, much more. Many businesses start with a good product or service but find there is simply not enough customers around who want them, with inevitable results as far as the business is concerned. It is therefore vital that before any venture goes ahead adequate market research is done to see if the project is likely to succeed.

This section therefore summarises the findings of the market research and specifically answers the following questions: a) how large is the market for your product or service and what assumptions are you making to arrive at the figures you present? b) what competition is there — names, details? c) what advantages do these competitors have? and d) what advantages do you have over your competitors — ie what makes you so special? All statements need to be backed up with figures gleaned from the market research. Remarks such as "There is a

large market for ..." without providing any figures are simply worthless.

This section should also outline the Marketing Plan, ie how you propose to advertise, promote, distribute and sell your product or service. To cover this aspect fully may in itself take a page or many more, and should answer the following questions: a) how will your product or service be promoted (full details and costs), b) how will your product or service be sold, ie retail, wholesale, agent, mail-order, export or whatever? and c) the planned phases of an expanding marketing operation (if appropriate).

Suppliers/Sub-contractors Many businesses rely on other businesses to supply them with their raw materials, stock, parts or services. Any problems in obtaining these can spell disaster for a venture, particularly a new one. On the other hand, some suppliers and sub-contractors knowing the importance of their customers provide generous support and credit facilities.

Be careful of "single-sourcing" which is when you rely heavily on just one supplier. If possible you should have alternative suppliers. This section of the Business Plan therefore discusses which suppliers and sub-contractors you plan to use, mentions their company names and reports on discussions and correspondence with them.

Premises & Equipment:
Premises This section states the type of premises required (ie office, shop, warehouse, workshop, yard, factory...) and floor area necessary (usually in square feet). It also states the desired geographic location of the premises (giving reasons) and other requirements such as large loading

bays, concrete floors, three-phase electrical power etc. In some cases suitable premises might already have been found in which case this should be mentioned. It should also be stated whether the premises will be bought or rented and if it is expected that the premises will benefit from any government grants or other special financial assistance.

Equipment This section of the Plan notes what equipment is necessary, whether it will be purchased new or second-hand and from what source(s). Particularly where the equipment is expensive or extensive, it may be wise to list the equipment which is needed in an Appendix at the back of the Business Plan. You should also state whether the equipment is to be purchased outright or leased and if it is expected that there will be any government grants or other special financial assistance.

Transport A van or car is often required and frequently represents a significant proportion of the start-up and running costs. It therefore merits a statement or two describing what type of vehicle is required and what its function will be. State whether or not the vehicle will be purchased new or second-hand, bought or leased and its likely annual mileage (which will be reflected in the running costs shown in the Cashflow Forecast).

Legal Aspects:
Licence You would only include this paragraph if a licence was required to carry out the proposed venture and if so from whom such a licence is obtained, at what cost, what time delays are likely and what criteria have

Preparing the Business Plan

to be met before one can obtain such a licence.

Planning Permission Again you would include this paragraph if it was relevant, in which case comments should be made on any likely time delay and discussions to date with the relevant planning authority.

Patents Where relevant this aspect should be mentioned.

General Any relevant laws or regulations which have a significant effect on the business could be mentioned here together with a comment as to what effect they have or could have.

Financial:

Pricing This section specifies your pricing policy. Importers, wholesalers and retailers should mention their proposed "mark-up". Manufacturers should mention their "mark-up" or "margin". Service businesses should mention their proposed hourly rates.

$$\text{Mark-up} = \frac{(\text{selling price} - \text{cost price})}{\text{cost price}} \times 100\%$$

$$\text{Margin} = \frac{(\text{selling price} - \text{cost price})}{\text{selling price}} \times 100\%$$

It is usual to mention the norms of your industry. The prices you use are crucial, especially as new businesses often under-price, with dire results.

Cashflow Forecast In some respects this could be classed as the "heart" of the Business Plan as it embodies, in figures, much of what the plan discusses in words. The Cashflow Forecast is just what it says — a forecast of cash flowing in and out of the business (on a monthly basis). This is normally for 12 months ahead (though

a project with long lead times may need a 24 or 36 month forecast). The preparation of the Cashflow requires:
a) estimates and assumptions which should be clearly stated in the text and
b) hard facts from your research.

Any grants or special financial assistance should be noted here. If the one-off start-up costs are significant, as in the attached example, these should be listed in a separate Appendix at the back of the Business Plan.

The golden rule with Cashflow Forecasts is to be pessimistic and in particular not to underestimate your overheads which always seem to become larger than anticipated. Also, it takes time for a business to establish itself and therefore the monthly sales figures should reflect this (with any seasonal variations, such as high Christmas sales, superimposed).

Due to the importance of preparing a Cashflow Forecast, it is covered in more detail at the end of this chapter.

Projected P & L (Profit & Loss Account). This is also called a "Forecast Profit & Loss Account" or abbreviated to a "Forecast P & L". It would normally be prepared by your accountant and be attached near the end of the Business Plan. It is an important summary indicating the likely overheads the business will face and the profit it should make.

Projected Balance Sheet This is required for any larger project, say one requiring start-up capital of more than about £20,000.

Project Risk Assessment Every venture has risk which must be quantified wherever possible. You must assess the risk and equally any potential

Every venture has a risk factor....

backer will be interested to know this as their money is at stake. Potential risk could come from a number of sources — a new competitor, changes in legislation, difficulties in obtaining stock or raw materials, changes in overseas conditions and currency exchange fluctuations, sickness, a bad fire or flood ... A more mundane (and common) risk is simply the expected level of turnover is not achieved.

A useful exercise is to do a second Cashflow Forecast assuming 20% (or 50%) less sales while the "overheads" (ie wages, rent, rates, heat, light, phone etc) all remain the same. This could be commented upon in this section with the new (low sales) Cashflow Forecast attached as an Appendix at the end of the Plan. You should also in this section

Preparing the Business Plan

comment on any contingency plans you have to meet setbacks such as who would take over if you became ill.

Financial Requirements This is usually the last paragraph and it should state in clear unequivocal terms the total money the project needs, how much you are putting in and if any loans are required. Loan requirements should be split into share capital (for a limited company), bank loans and overdraft facilities, and when this money is required. In addition you should state in broad terms what the borrowed money is to be used for.

Appendices These are found at the back of the Business Plan. Appendices can include:

Cashflow Forecast ... essential.

Forecast P&L ... desirable for small projects, essential for others.

Projected Balance Sheet ... ditto.

Trading Accounts ... only if taking over a firm or expanding yours.

Technical Data ... where appropriate.

Market Research ... where done independently or if lengthy.

Sales Literature, Leaflets, Photos ... ...where available.

CASHFLOW FORECASTS

THE LAYOUT

This section refers to the blank Cashflow Forecast (see later) and the worked example Cashflow Forecast (prepared for the fictitious fashion shop we've called "Simply Perfect") which is at the end of this chapter.

If you now refer to the worked example cashflow (on page 44), note that each vertical column represents one month and glancing down the left side the lines are numbered 1 to 31.

Line Headings Note that the horizontal lines 1 to 4 list all cash "in" (ie all the money paid in or received by the business) and lines 6 to 27 list all cash "out" (ie expenses paid by the business). Note too that these line headings are not rigid — use headings appropriate to your venture.

Top Line: This gives the 12 months starting with May in the case of the worked example. At the end of the line is a column for the TOTALS.

Line 1 (SALES (inc VAT)): This is the most crucial line as you have to estimate your likely sales (called "Turnover") for the year ahead. The assumptions you make should be clearly stated in the text of the Business Plan. With almost all businesses you have to build up your trade and so there should be a gradual build-up from a low monthly sales figure to a plateau which can be anywhere from months 6-18 for a shop or a year or much more if it is a manufacturing business with long lead-times. There could also be monthly seasonal variations. If you are offering credit, you should show the payments in the month when you expect to receive the cash.

Break-even In a situation where it is almost impossible to forecast your SALES, then you could do a "break-even" cashflow, ie you would complete the whole cashflow form leaving the SALES line until the very end and then you insert what SALES you have to make to break-even (in practical terms this means ensuring the bottom line of the cashflow remains positive or

within your overdraft limit).

In every Business Plan it is most important to explain how the predicted sales figure was arrived at. See the worked example for the shop "Simply Perfect" to see how it was done in that particular case.

One of the most common errors people make when completing their first Cashflow Forecast is that they wildly over-estimate their forecast monthly sales figures.

Line 2 (LOANS): This line is for bank loans or any other loans.

Line 3 (OWNERS CAPITAL): This is for the capital you put into the business.

Line 4 (OTHER MONEY IN): Any other sources of finance such as a VAT repayment (if your "input" tax exceeds your "output" tax — see the chapter **Coping With Taxation**), payments from Enterprise Allowance and any grants.

Line 5 (TOTAL): Lines 1 + 2 + 3 + 4.

Line 6 (STOCK/RAW MATERIALS): On this line you list the stock or materials you have to buy (including VAT). In many cases there will be an initial "stocking-up" phase. Secondly the stock should bear a relationship to the SALES line, eg if you have a 100% mark-up then if you buy an item for £10 you sell it for £20 and the ratio between the cash SALES line and the STOCK line should be about 2:1 and this is what is shown in the example cashflow from September onwards. So notice that when £3000 of stock is sold in September we assume £1500 of new stock arrives in September and is paid for. If you were enjoying 30 days credit

from your suppliers then the stock might arrive one month but would not be paid for until the following month and this can have a marked bearing on your cashflow. Try it yourself and notice that with, say 30 days credit, your own cash requirements to set up a business are reduced.

Line 7 (ADVERTISING & PROMOTION): Here is listed expenditure on adverts and promotion.

Line 8 (BANK CHARGES/INTEREST): Bank charges are often quarterly and vary greatly depending on your usage of your bank account. If your cashflow shows an overdraft requirement, to get a quick (and approximate) estimate of interest charges, take the interest as 1% per month, so in our example where the overdraft for the first 3 months is -£1150, -£1505 and -£1709, then the quarterly interest charge is approx: £11.50 + £15.05 + £17.09 = £44.

Line 9 (BUSINESS INSURANCE): The sample cashflow shows business insurance of £350.

Line 10 (DRAWINGS/SALARIES/NI): Here you list your "Drawings", ie the "wages" you (and any partners) take out of the business. For a limited company this is called a "salary". Include here also the National Insurance (NI) contributions and for salaries, PAYE.

Line 11 (ELECTRIC/GAS/HEAT): This line is for any electricity bills (and/or gas, oil, coal). Check with your local Electricity/Gas offices as to how often the bills are issued, ie monthly, every second month or quarterly?

Line 12 (FEES): On this line would be listed any legal, accountancy or other fees (eg surveyor).

Line 13 (HP/LEASE/LOAN PAYMENTS): This line is for HP or Lease payments if you are purchasing vehicles or equipment on HP or leasing them. The line is also for loan repayments so is related directly to line 2. Most smaller bank loans are repaid by fixed monthly amounts over a 2 or 3 year period. Interest rates can vary greatly, but as an example assume 14% fixed interest, then the repayments would be:

£1,000 loan over 3 years —
monthly repayments approx £40

£2,000 loan over 3 years —
monthly repayments approx £80

£5,000 loan over 3 years —
monthly repayments approx £200

Line 14 (MOTOR – FUEL): This is separated from other motoring expenses as it can sometimes be useful to account for fuel usage separately.

Line 15 (MOTOR – OTHER EXPENSES): eg servicing, repairs, annual Tax disc and insurance.

Line 16 (POSTAGE/CARRIAGE).

Line 17 (RENT & RATES): Most commercial rents are paid monthly or quarterly in advance, and most local government authorities allow rates payments over a number of months as shown in the example.

Line 18 (REPAIRS & MAINTENANCE): This is for repairs to your premises (vehicles are covered at line 15).

Line 19 (STAFF WAGES): This line is for all wages you pay to staff.

Line 20 (STAFF PAYE/NI): Put Staff wage PAYE and National Insurance payments on this line. (Note your own NI contributions appear on line 10).

Line 21 (STATIONERY/PRINTING): Here you enter the costs of your stationery and the printing of your letterheads etc.

Line 22 (SUNDRIES): This is for all the little bits you will find you need!

Line 23 (TELEPHONE/FAX): Note that unless there is a working phone already in the premises, BT usually make a "connection charge" plus rental in advance. A new user may also have to pay a deposit which is refundable.

Line 24 (TRAVELLING): This is for costs incurred while travelling in the course of doing your business (eg on sales trips or attending trade shows or meetings away from your office).

Line 25 (VAT): A small business may not need to register for VAT unless its turnover exceeds the current threshold figure (see the **Tax Data Page** at the end of the book). Our fictitious shop "Simply Perfect" has not registered for VAT as its projected first year's turnover is less than the current VAT registration threshold. So line 25 remains zero.

For a VAT registered business, line 25 is used for the VAT payments made to Customs & Excise. If all the sales of the business are chargeable for VAT then to calculate line 25, the VAT due = VAT included in SALES (line 1) less VAT included in STOCK (line 6) less VAT in any other expenses (eg phone bills) over the same trading period (usually 3 months).

	CASH IN										
1	Sales (inc VAT)										1
2	Bank or other Loans										2
3	Owner's Capital										3
4	Other Money In										4
5	TOTAL										5
	CASH OUT (inc VAT)										
6	Stock/Raw Materials										6
7	Advertising & Promotion										7
8	Bank Charges/Interest										8
9	Business Insurance										9
10	Drawings/Salaries/NI										10
11	Electric/Gas/Heat										11
12	Fees (eg Accountant, Lawyer)										12
13	HP/Lease/Loan Payments										13
14	Motor — Fuel										14
15	— Other Expenses										15
16	Postage/Carriage										16
17	Rent & Rates										17
18	Repairs & Maintenance										18
19	Staff Wages										19
20	Staff PAYE/NI										20
21	Stationery/Printing										21
22	Sundries										22
23	Telephone/Fax										23
24	Travelling										24
25	VAT										25
26	Other Expenses										26
27	CAPITAL EXPENDITURE										27
28	TOTAL										28
29	Net Cashflow										29
30	Opening Balance										30
31	CLOSING BALANCE										31

			TOTALS
1			
2			
3			
4			
5			
6			
7			
8			
9			
10			
11			
12			
13			
14			
15			
16			
17			
18			
19			
20			
21			
22			
23			
24			
25			
26			
27			
28			
29			
30			
31			

© 1991 P. Hingston

Line 26 (OTHER EXPENSES): This line is for any expenses which do not come under the categories listed above. You may wish to have several such lines on your own Cashflow.

Line 27 (CAPITAL EXPENDITURE): "Capital expenditure" covers once-off purchases of tangible assets such as vehicles, machinery, tools, office equipment, buildings (including alterations) etc. They tend to have a big effect on your cashflow but since the timing of such purchases are under your control, the Cashflow Forecast can help you decide when to make a purchase.

Line 28 (TOTAL): This totals lines 6 to 27 and represents the total cash outflow for each month.

Line 29 (NET CASHFLOW): This is line 5 minus line 28. If the figure is positive it means that more cash was received than was spent during the month – good. If negative, more cash was spent than received – not good!

Line 30 (OPENING BALANCE): This always starts at 0 for a new business, and each month equals the CLOSING BALANCE of the previous month.

Line 31 (CLOSING BALANCE): This is the sum of line 29 and line 30 and represents the forecast cash in the bank at the end of each month which is of singular importance! If this line is negative, it means your bank account is overdrawn. Is it within your overdraft limits?
Note: Remember the bottom line of a Cashflow Forecast is not a "profit" or a "loss". Also, to distinguish between money from sales and money from loans (or your capital input), you might move lines 2 to 4 to *below* line 29, so the "Net Cashflow" reflects the actual trading position.

Procedure For Completing A Cashflow Forecast

Complete the form as follows (in pencil to allow changes), omit the £ signs and exclude pence:

1. Working ACROSS the sheet, write in the months (top line).
2. Now for the first month, fill in the SALES (line 1), unless you are doing a "break-even" cashflow in which case this comes at the very end.
3. Miss out line 2 at this stage, but fill in lines 3, 4 and 5.
4. Fill in lines 6 to 28, missing out lines 8, 10, and 13 (also 25 if not VAT-reg'd).
5. Now take line 28 from line 5 to get line 29 and add lines 29 + 30 to get 31.
6. Repeat this for the whole year. You will almost certainly have a lot of negative figures in line 31 (if not, you do not need a loan and lines 2 and 13 will remain zero). Assuming your line 31 figures are negative, try to estimate how much money you need for capital expenditure (this would normally be funded by a loan, HP or lease) while stock/raw materials would normally be funded by an overdraft. The cashflow should indicate a diminishing overdraft requirement.
7. Put any loan requirement figure into line 2 and check the sum of that amount and the overdraft does not exceed your line 3 as, remember, banks prefer not to put more money than you do into a project. Now fill in lines 8 and 13.
8. Now you can see what drawings (line 10) the business can support.

Note: Doing Cashflow Forecasts by hand takes time and care. A small computer can allow you to do it much more easily. See the chapter **Using a Computer**.

<u>Miss Joan Smith</u>

<u>T/A SIMPLY PERFECT</u>

<u>BUSINESS PLAN</u>

Home Address:

12, Glasgow Street
Greenock
Tel: Greenock (0475) 323

Author's Note: Please remember this is a fictitious Business Plan included to illustrate how such a plan might be written and presented. Your own Business Plan should be written in your own words and should incorporate your own data and figures.

SUMMARY

Nature of Business   :   Retail shop (Ladies outerwear fashion for the over 50s)

Location   :   Greenock

Proprietor   :   Miss Joan Smith

Staff   :   Proprietor only

Market   :   The main market is ladies, over 50, living in Greenock
                         (population: 66,500). The nearest shops catering specifically
                         for this market are in Paisley, 18 miles distant.

Premises Required   :   About 500 sq ft in a good location

Proposed Shop Name   :   Simply Perfect

Turnover   :   First year estimate approx £34,500
                         Second year estimate approx £40,000

Financing   :   Depending upon which shop is rented, capital of approximately
                         £10,500 is required of which the proprietor can raise £6,500
                         leaving a balance of £4,000 to be found. A 3-year bank loan of
                         £2,000 would be sufficient with in addition an overdraft facility
                         of £2,000 to allow for stock purchases in the initial months.

39

INTRODUCTION

The objective is to set up a ladies outerwear fashion shop in the town centre of Greenock. The purpose of this Plan is to raise the finance for the venture.

PERSONNEL

Management.   The shop will be under the direct supervision of the proprietor, Miss Joan Smith. After working as a primary school teacher, Miss Smith, age 42, has spent 7 years in the retail trade, initially as a shop assistant and more recently as Assistant Manageress of the Miss Jones boutique in Gourock. Miss Smith owns her own flat. She plans to attend evening courses on elementary book-keeping at the local College.

Staff.   Miss Smith does not plan to employ any staff. However her sister, who lives locally and has experience of working in shops, is able to assist her should the need arise.

SERVICE

Service Description.   The shop will stock ladies outerwear aimed mainly at the over 50s age group. Garments will include dresses, skirts, blouses, overcoats, raincoats, hosiery, hats and accessories and will be in styles and sizes appropriate to that age group.

Market Research & Marketing Plan.   Miss Smith has observed during her years in retail in the area that many of her older clientele complained that they were obliged to travel to Paisley, some 18 miles away, to find good clothes shops to suit them. This prompted Miss Smith to investigate the market further. The population of Greenock is 66,500 but it is a spread out town adjoining two other towns, Gourock to the west and Port Glasgow to the east, thus the potential market is larger than just that of Greenock itself. The existing shops in the area which might present competition to her venture are as follows:

Icebergs	A large Department store catering to a wide age group with a limited range for the over 50s.
Inver-Fashions	A new upmarket shop but with relatively high prices and fashions more appropriate to younger customers.
Miss Jones	A small boutique with only skirts and dresses for this age group.

At present therefore there is little direct competition from stores in Greenock or its neighbouring towns, Gourock and Port Glasgow. The main competition are the stores in Paisley which these ladies visit.

Miss Smith has questioned a sample of 50 ladies who she knows and who would all be potential customers of her new store. Of these 44 said they would at least consider a shop locally in preference to one 18 miles away in Paisley. The only reservations were expressed by 6 ladies whose work took them to Paisley anyway and so they would continue to visit the shops there.

To promote the shop the proprietor plans to organise fashion shows at the local Ladies Luncheon Club and the Tuesday Club. She will also advertise these special events in the local newspaper and monitor the response carefully. She would also change the shop window weekly as she believes that is an important way to promote her stock.

Suppliers. Miss Smith has attended two national fashion trade shows and has spoken to 15 potential suppliers who carry appropriate lines and they have almost all stated that they would normally offer 30 days credit on receipt of satisfactory references. This credit is not reflected in the Cashflow as the suppliers stated that this credit facility would only come into effect after an initial order or two had been placed and paid for satisfactorily.

PREMISES & EQUIPMENT

Premises. A shop to rent of around 500 sq ft is required sited preferably on West Street or Regent Crescent, possibly Hill Lane. These are near the town centre but do not attract the very high rents of Main Street. There are two vacant shops which may be suitable and the Cashflow Forecast reflects the rent and rates of the shop at 12 Regent Crescent. This shop is available on a 7 year lease (with rent and rates of £6,500 pa). Although this site is on the edge of the prime town centre shopping area, it is situated between the main car park and the town centre shops, so many people walk by.

Equipment. Certain equipment (some purchased second-hand) would be required. In addition the shop at 12 Regent Crescent would require its interior repainted, the exterior being satisfactory though a new shop sign would be required. The start-up capital expenditure costs are listed as an Appendix to this Business Plan.

Transport. The business does not require transport and so Miss Smith does not plan to purchase a vehicle. Stock ordered by her at trade shows or through suppliers Reps will be despatched to the shop by normal parcel delivery services.

LEGAL ASPECTS

The situation regarding Planning Permission has been investigated with the local authorities. Since the intention is to trade from premises which have recently been used for similar retailing purposes Miss Smith has been informed that no application for Planning Permission is required.

FINANCIAL

Pricing. Garments and accessories in the shop will reflect the mark-ups typical of the fashion trade locally which are 80% to 120%.

Cashflow Forecast. The attached Cashflow Forecast shows a turnover in the first year of £34,500 at which the business is just above break-even, but it is thought that by the second full year of operation the turnover will rise to around £40,000. The sales estimates are based on two different calculations which both arrive at a minimum turnover of around £35,000. In the first method Miss Smith has estimated her proposed shop's first year's sales to be 75% of that done by the boutique Miss Jones where she worked recently. Second, she has calculated the likely turnover in terms of the Rate of Stock Turn which is defined as the turnover divided by the stock value (at retail prices). Hence a stock value of £14,000* and a turnover of £35,000 would give a Rate of Stock Turn of 2.5 which should be obtainable.

It is also assumed that there will be Solicitor's fees of £300 for arranging the lease on the shop, insurance has been quoted at £350 and accountant's fees of £400 have been allowed for.

Project Risk Assessment. It is Miss Smith's opinion that the local market can sustain another specialist shop in addition to her proposed venture so that should a second shop open at some future date her project would not be jeopardised. If sales were 20% less than forecast, the business would survive, albeit with difficulty. Finally, should Miss Smith take ill, her sister would run the shop.

Financial Requirements. Depending upon which store is rented, approximately £10,500 capital is required of which the proprietor can raise £6,500. A 3-year bank loan of £2,000 would pay for setting up costs (mainly equipment), while an overdraft of £2,000 would assist with the provision of stock.

*Author's Note: In this example, £14,000 at retail prices is stock valued at around £7,000. You will notice from the worked example cashflow that in May the shop purchases £5,000 of stock. Over the next few months the stock level rises as monthly purchases exceed sales.

START-UP CAPITAL EXPENDITURE

Fixtures & Fittings

Shelving	£150.00
Display Units	£290.00
Exterior Shop Sign	£250.00
Repaint Shop Interior	£150.00
Additional Lighting	£100.00
Mirrors (for changing room)	£ 30.00
Curtains (for changing room)	£ 80.00

Equipment

2nd Hand Cash Till	£200.00
Pricing Gun	£ 50.00
2nd Hand Mannequin	£100.00
Clothes Hangers	£ 50.00
TOTAL:	£1450.00

PROJECTED PROFIT & LOSS ACCOUNT

SALES	£34,500 [1]
LESS COST OF SALES	£17,250 [2]
GROSS PROFIT	£17,250

LESS EXPENSES: [3]

Advertising & Promotion	£ 400
Bank Interest	£ 91
Business Insurance	£ 350
Electricity/Gas/Heat	£ 575
Fees	£ 700
Loan Interest	£ 269 [4]
Motor	£ 0
Postage/Carriage	£ 0
Rent & Rates	£6500
Repairs & Maintenance	£ 200
Staff Wages	£ 0
Stationery/Printing	£ 40
Sundries	£ 260
Telephone/Fax	£ 600
Travelling	£ 200
Depreciation: [5]	
Fixtures & Fittings	£ 262
Equipment	£ 100
	£10,547

NET PROFIT	£ 6,703 [6]

Author's Notes:
(1) If VAT-registered, Sales = Turnover (ie Total Sales) less VAT.
(2) In this case, this equals the value of stock sold which produced the £34,500 sales. Estimated here using an average mark-up of 100%. (To get this figure at year end, one would add up all stock purchased and deduct the value of stock in the shop after the last day of trading in the financial year).
(3) If VAT-registered, all these figures are less any VAT charged.
(4) Only the interest is tax deductible. Here the £2000 loan is repaid in 36 months at £80/month (obviously this rate can vary), so there is interest of:
[(£80 x 36) – £2000] ÷ 36 = £24.44/month x 11 months this year.
(5) See note on depreciation on page 11.
(6) The Net Profit needs to equal or exceed the Proprietor's Drawings (allowing for National Insurance contributions and any Income Tax that may be due).
(General) Capital Expenditure, Proprietors Drawings and Vehicle Purchase costs would not appear on the P & L Account as they are not tax deductible items.
(General) This is a simplified P & L to illustrate the main features. For instance, it omits bank charges. In practice you also usually have "accruals". This is because your financial year will not coincide exactly with the periods for rent, rates, phone rental etc, but you must take these into account, as part of these liabilities relate to the financial year covered by the P & L.

CASHFLOW FORECAST

	CASH IN	MAY	JUN	JUL	AUG	SEP	OCT	NOV	DEC	JAN	FEB	MAR	APR	TOTALS
1	Sales (inc VAT)	1000	1500	2000	3000	3000	2750	4000	8000	1500	1750	2750	3250	34500
2	Bank or other Loans		2000											2000
3	Owner's Capital	6500												6500
4	Other Money In													
5	TOTAL	7500	3500	2000	3000	3000	2750	4000	8000	1500	1750	2750	3250	43000
	CASH OUT (inc VAT)													
6	Stock/Raw Materials	5000	3000	1500	1250	1500	1375	2000	4000	750	875	1375	1625	24250
7	Advertising & Promotion	200						200						400
8	Bank Charges/Interest			44			38			9				91
9	Business Insurance	350												350
10	Drawings/Salaries/NI		300	300	300	500	500	500	800	700	700	700	700	6000
11	Electric/Gas/Heat		75		75		75		125		125		100	575
12	Fees (eg Accountant, Lawyer)	300											400	700
13	HP/Lease/Loan Payments		80	80	80	80	80	80	80	80	80	80	80	880
14	Motor – Fuel													
15	– Other Expenses													
16	Postage/Carriage													
17	Rent & Rates	1000	250	250	1250	250	250	1250	250	250	1250	250		6500
18	Repairs & Maintenance		50			50			50			50		200
19	Staff Wages													
20	Staff PAYE/NI													
21	Stationery/Printing	20						20						40
22	Sundries	80	50	30	20	10	10	10	10	10	10	10	10	260
23	Telephone/Fax	250	50			100			100			100		600
24	Travelling					100							100	200
25	VAT													
26	Other Expenses													
27	CAPITAL EXPENDITURE	1450												1450
28	TOTAL	8650	3855	2204	2975	2590	2328	4060	5415	1799	3040	2565	3015	42496
29	Net Cashflow	(1150)	(355)	(204)	25	410	422	(60)	2585	(299)	(1290)	185	235	504
30	Opening Balance	0	(1150)	(1505)	(1709)	(1684)	(1274)	(852)	(912)	1673	1374	84	269	0
31	CLOSING BALANCE	(1150)	(1505)	(1709)	(1684)	(1274)	(852)	(912)	1673	1374	84	269	504	504

© 1991 P. Hingston

Author's Note: The Cashflow Forecast has been shown reduced in size to fit this page. Figures in brackets are negative, ie the business bank account would be in overdraft.

Raising the Finance

HOW MUCH MONEY DO YOU NEED?

Hopefully this question would have been answered while you were putting together the Business Plan. Basically what you should know is how much money you will need for:

a) Start-Up Capital   This is the money for the one-off start-up costs such as buying machinery or vehicles, developing or launching a product, fitting out a shop, equipping an office etc.

b) Working Capital   This is the short-term borrowing requirement which is usually caused by the following: the time delay between you buying something and reselling it (as in a shop) or the delay between providing a service and being paid for it or the delay between buying raw materials and selling the finished product.

The amount of money that you can raise has certain limits which are discussed below. If you cannot raise the money that the Business Plan indicates is necessary, then you either have to scale down the project, change the concept or you may even have to abandon it altogether.

If you start on a small scale and your business is profitable then you should be able to attract increased finance for expansion at the appropriate time.

SOURCES OF FINANCE

Almost certainly to raise the money to start the business will require funds from a number of sources.

In virtually every case, one or more of the Proprietors or Directors will have to put up a reasonable proportion of the funds required.

Your local Enterprise Agency, business development unit or accountant can advise you which banks and financiers you should approach.

The various options are as follows:

1. Yourself!
2. Friends and Relatives.
3. The "High Street" Banks.
4. Government.
5. Equity Financiers (for a Limited Company only).
6. HP/Leasing Firms.
7. Trade Credit.
8. Other Sources.

Each of these are now considered in turn...

1. YOURSELF

This is obviously the first place to look for money to start your own business. In addition to any spare cash you may have in the bank, building society or as shares you can also raise money by selling possessions.

Setting up a business can involve considerable sacrifice and a drop in living standards until the business is established. Typical "luxury" possessions that could be sold to raise cash include: stereos, photographic equipment, video recorders, colour TVs, jewellery, caravans, dinghies, premium bonds and so on.

Another possibility if you own a newish car is to sell it and buy a cheaper older one (or a van if that was better suited to the proposed venture), but obviously if your intended business involved a lot of driving then purchasing an old high-mileage vehicle may be unwise.

If larger sums of money are necessary you could consider selling your house (assuming you own it of course) and buying a more modest home — though check first what the legal expenses might add up to as that may cancel out the gain. A better idea may be to have a second mortgage on your existing home. This is only possible if the property is worth considerably more than the existing mortgage, allowing scope for the second mortgage on the unmortgaged part of the house value. Note though that second mortgages tend to be expensive.

A final, cautionary point is if you need to borrow large sums of money, almost certainly you will be asked for personal guarantees, ie should the venture fail, you will be called upon to honour the debt which may bankrupt you or make you homeless!

KEY POINT   Read the small print of any personal guarantee, get legal advice and consider this very carefully indeed.

Other points to note:

Situation: No Funds   If you have either no money or can only contribute a very small portion of the total required, then you may have difficulty in raising the balance simply because potential financial backers such as banks do not like to feel they are taking the lion's share of the risk. An alternative to money is capital you can introduce by way of machinery, plant, vehicles, equipment and even business premises, however modest.

Situation: Enough Personal Funds In contrast if you have sufficient personal funds to finance the complete project yourself, you might not think of talking to your bank, accountant or any other financial specialist. In some ways this

DIFFERENT FINANCIAL PACKAGES

Unless you are funding the new project entirely yourself, there are a number of ways in which the necessary finance can be put together. The process usually becomes ever more complex as the sums of money increase. The diagrams below should give you an idea of the typical financial packages to raise capital from £1,000 up to £250,000 or more.

Case I

In the case of a very small project requiring, say under £2,000, and where the proprietor has no capital, a bank may be prepared to provide an overdraft, particularly if there is adequate security. Being on an Enterprise scheme with a guaranteed regular allowance might help encourage a bank to lend money.

O/DRAFT

Case II

This is a very typical situation, where the proprietor raises the start-up capital (possibly by borrowing from friends and relatives) and the bank provides an overdraft to meet the working capital requirements of the business.

YOUR CAPITAL   **O/DRAFT**

Case III

Where there is a grant available the maximum likely bank funding may be increased. (In this case as a bank loan).

BANK LOAN   **GRANTS**   **YOUR CAPITAL**   **O/DRAFT**

Case IV

This is another typical situation, where the proprietor puts up at least half the necessary money with the bank providing the rest, partly as a short-term loan and partly as an overdraft.

BANK LOAN   **YOUR CAPITAL**   **O/DRAFT**

Case V

In the case of a franchise, a bank may be prepared to lend up to 60% or even 70% of the capital requirements.

BANK LOAN   **YOUR CAPITAL**   **O/DRAFT**

Case VI

This package is for a limited company with an outside investor, possibly a venture capitalist if the project is in the £50,000+ league.

BANK LOAN   **INVESTOR**   **YOUR CAPITAL**   **O/DRAFT**

can be a disadvantage because one misses out on the considerable expertise of these people. Also, because you do not have to convince would-be lenders of the viability of your project you may not prepare as conscientious a Business Plan. It is recommended that you always prepare a Business Plan and ask your bank and accountant to read it through and comment. If they express doubts, then you should take another very hard look at the venture and do not be so sure that it is going to work.

2. FRIENDS & RELATIVES

Many people shy away from this good source of money. Care is however required to avoid family friction — select only those people who could afford to lose what you are asking, then show them your Business Plan, ask them for a specific amount and do mention that you do not expect an immediate reply as you would like them to think it over. They can help fund your venture in any (or a combination) of the following ways:

Loan (Interest Free) This is usually reserved for loans made by close family or possibly a very close friend. The loan normally being repaid within months rather than years.

Loan (With Interest) For situations other than that mentioned above it is more appropriate that interest is added. For convenience use a fixed rate of interest based on the average "bank base rate" taken over the previous 12 months (this is to avoid artificial peaks and troughs in the rate). Choosing the bank base rate as the interest figure to use is useful for it not only saves argument but it is also cheaper for the would-be borrower (as

banks normally charge more than base rate) and it is also often a better rate of interest than the lender would get from simply putting the money in a bank or building society. Note you may get tax relief on the interest you have to pay.

"Sleeping Partner" Whereas with a loan your friends or relatives would not normally have any "say" in the running of your business, in this case the money is invested as risk capital and although the lender may not do the day-to-day work, he or she should certainly have a say in how the business is run. As a partner they should be aware of their liability for any debts the business may build up. As a "sleeping partner" they should not draw a wage as such for they are not doing the day-to-day work, instead they should take a proportion of the net profits of the business (ie profit after all overheads and your agreed "drawings" have been deducted) at the end of the financial year.

One suggestion is the division of profits could be in the same ratio as the capital originally invested in the business, ie if you put £3,000 into the business at the start and the "sleeping partner" puts in £5,000 then you could share the profits as $\frac{3}{8}$ to yourself and $\frac{5}{8}$ to your partner. In addition you should have a "wage".

For a Limited Company Only In this case the lender could opt to invest in the business by buying shares (refer also to **5. EQUITY FINANCIERS** below). Note that in a limited company, he who holds the majority shareholding can dictate how the company will be run! This is unlike a partnership where (unless the Partnership Agreement states to the contrary) the partners have an equal say in the running of the

business even if their capital contributions vary.

If your friends or relatives agree to help fund your business it is essential that whatever is agreed is put down in writing. Unless the money is a very small loan, the document should be drafted by a solicitor. The document should clearly specify: a) the amount of the loan, b) when the loan is to be repaid (be realistic here), c) how the loan is to be repaid if the business runs into trouble (usually the repayment period is extended), d) what interest (if any) is to be paid, e) to what extent the lender can interfere with the business (usually not at all in the case of a loan), f) who the money should be repaid to in the event of death of the lender and g) what should happen if the business ceases to trade. In the case of a "sleeping partner" the loan conditions could be detailed in the Partnership Agreement, and in the case of shares in a limited company the Memorandum and Articles of Association could cover these conditions.

3. THE "HIGH STREET" BANKS

Banks are in the business of lending money so they are constantly on the look-out for good business propositions in which to invest. The so-called "High Street" Clearing Banks have over the last few years become much more interested in the small business sector. One must say, however, that new businesses present a considerable risk so banks are naturally cautious. They will want to know full details of the proposed business and the people behind the project. The Business Plan you will have prepared is precisely the document for that purpose.

In addition to reading the Business Plan the bank manager may be keen to

Raising the Finance

meet not only the people behind the plan but also their spouses and accountants. For although a carefully prepared Business Plan is important the banker knows that should things go wrong it will be the calibre of the people behind the project and the support they get from their spouses and advisors that will count towards redeeming the project and preventing a complete failure.

Shared Risk   Banks prefer the risk of a new venture to be shared and rarely like to put up more than 50% of the capital. In the case of franchises, with any well-known franchise company, the banks are sometimes prepared to lend up to 60% or even 70% of the total capital requirements, provided of course that the projected profits of the business can sustain the loan repayments. This generous attitude to selected franchises is simply because of their proven success rate, but it should be pointed out that taking on a franchise requires a certain minimum of capital, depending upon the actual franchise, and it can be an expensive though possibly safer way to start in business.

Loans & Overdrafts   "Loans" are made normally to finance the purchase of the fixed assets of the business (ie plant, equipment and buildings). These loans can be at either fixed or variable rates of interest and are repaid either monthly or quarterly over a pre-agreed "term", usually 2-5 + years (longer for buildings).

"Overdrafts" in contrast are for short-term working capital. This can bridge the gap: a) between buying stock and reselling it; b) providing a service (particularly to trade customers) and waiting up to 30, 60 or even 90 days to be paid; or c) buying raw materials and selling the manufactured product. An overdraft, if granted, will be for an agreed amount (Note: *Never* exceed this limit without prior permission from the bank manager, because the facility can be withdrawn at any time if the bank thinks you are mishandling your financial affairs).

An overdraft is usually the cheapest money you can borrow (other than special government subsidised loans — see below) as you only pay interest on the daily balance "in the red", this interest usually having to be repaid quarterly.

Many businesses require a combination of loan and overdraft facilities when they start up. All banks publish and display their "Base Lending Rate" — as a small business you will normally pay several % more for your loan or overdraft. Ensure you know what rate you are going to be charged and remember it is negotiable!

(Government) Loan Guarantee Scheme   This is a scheme whereby the government takes some of the risk in backing small business. It does this by underwriting 70% of the loan so the bank risks only 30% of the total borrowed. In Inner City Task Force Areas, the government underwrites 85%. (These rates are under review).

There is a small premium but in practice the repayments can be similar to a normal business loan. The scheme is suitable for a promising and well-researched venture where the entrepreneur cannot provide adequate security against a conventional bank loan and there is no track record.

Security   Although you should not start by offering security, a bank will normally request this to cover any loan should the business fail. In any event you should not agree to security in excess of the value of loan you are requesting. Types of security include:

a) Guarantors This is where someone else with suitable personal or business assets guarantees to pay the bank should you default.

b) Your Home (if you own it!) Where the market value of the house less the outstanding mortgage is substantial in comparison to the size of loan requested then a home can provide useful and non-onerous security. Where this is not the case then it is best not offered nor accepted for security due to the unnecessary additional strain on the entrepreneur and his or her family. The bank is able, and will, foreclose on the mortgage in the event of a business failing, no matter how small the amount owed, and the borrower will lose his or her home.

c) Your Work Premises In contrast, if you own your shop, office or workshop, this could be excellent security.

d) Life Assurance Policies This applies primarily to those policies with a surrender value.

e) (For a Limited Company only) The two commonly used forms of security in this context are *Directors' personal guarantees* where the Directors pledge to pay up from their personal funds should the business be unable to make the loan repayments. This effectively removes one of the advantages of forming a company and the limited liability protection it offers. If personal guarantees are sought, read the small print carefully and take legal advice. The second commonly used form of security is the *floating charge* where

the bank has rights over the assets of a company as these change (ie float) up and down as, for instance, stock levels vary.

Life Insurance Depending upon your age, the size of loan you require and what other security is offered, a bank may require a life insurance policy to be payable to the bank to cover its loan should you die prematurely.

Shopping Around If you do not get what you require or the conditions attached are unacceptable then it is worth shopping around. If a bank turns you down, ask why – it may be the project is simply too risky and you would be wise to modify or abandon it.

4. GOVERNMENT

It makes good sense for anyone setting up in business to fully explore what government grants, "soft" loans, subsidies or other assistance is available. Government help comes from many sources (the EC, Central and Local Government) and is channelled through many different bodies. It can also vary considerably from one area of the country to another.

In addition to the various specific schemes outlined on the following pages, there is sometimes local assistance which as a general guide provides help under the following broad categories:

Premises Several incentives relate to premises but these are mainly (not exclusively) available for manufacturing businesses. Such incentives include rent-free periods (which can be several months, possibly up to 2 years) or stepped rents, reduced rates, and

	Development Area		Intermediate Area

Enterprise Zone	Expiry Date
Dudley (2)	10.1994
Lr Swansea Valley (2)	3.1995
N W Kent (2)	10.1996
Inverclyde	3.1999
Sunderland	4.2000
N Lanarkshlre	2.2003

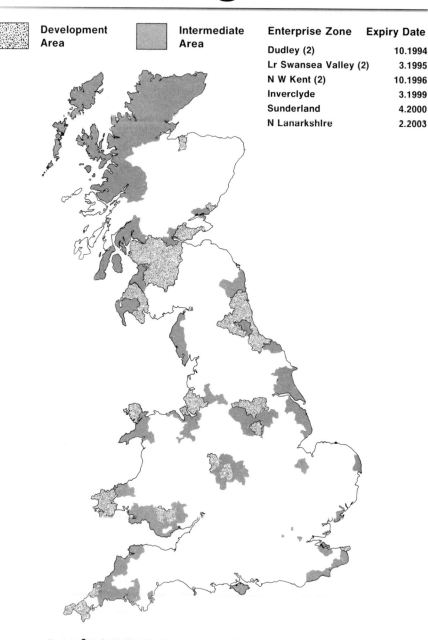

Assisted Areas (from August 1993)

Raising the Finance

sometimes grants towards paying for new buildings, extensions or renovation work.

Equipment Again, most incentives which relate to equipment are for manufacturing businesses.

Staff There are some schemes around to encourage the employment and training of staff. Where available these usually subsidise the wages of a new employee (ie pay a portion of the wage bill for a set time), provide a straight cash lump sum if one takes on staff or they pay wages during a set training period. There are also some special schemes to encourage the employment of long-term unemployed people, the disabled and youngsters.

The Enterprise Initiative The Government assistance to industry in Britain comes under the general heading of the "Enterprise Initiative". The various grants are summarised below but are more fully described in a free booklet titled the "Enterprise Initiative" available from the Department of Trade and Industry on tel: 0800 500 200. The booklet also lists the various contacts around Britain (Note: Northern Ireland has its own schemes). Initiatives of relevance to a small business trying to raise finance include:

Regional Selective Assistance As part of their "Regional" help, within the Development and Intermediate Areas (see map on previous page), Regional Selective Assistance is available on a discretionary basis. The grant is based on the amount of fixed capital required and the number of jobs likely to be created or safeguarded as a result.

Purely local consumer type services such as shops are likely to be excluded. The level of grant will be negotiated as the minimum necessary to ensure the project goes ahead so one must clearly demonstrate that without this support the project will not proceed. Thus application for this assistance must be before the project is started. There is a streamlined procedure when applying for grants less than £25,000.

Additionally access can be provided to competitively financed capital loans at fixed interest rates from the European Coal & Steel Community.

Regional Enterprise Grants There are two types of discretionary grant to help firms start, modernise, expand or diversify – the Regional Investment Grant & Regional Innovation Grant.

Regional Investment Grant This grant applies only to small firms employing fewer than 25 people in one of the Development Areas or the Intermediate Areas in Derbyshire, South Yorkshire and Plymouth.

"Investment" projects in most manufacturing and some service sectors are eligible for a grant of 15% (up to a maximum of £15,000) towards expenditure on plant and machinery (new or second-hand), buildings, purchase of land and site preparation, and vehicles used solely on site.

Again, you must demonstrate need for the grant and application must be before the project commences.

Regional Innovation Grant This grant is available for firms for projects leading to the development of new products or processes. To be eligible, a business must have fewer than 50 employees and be in a Development, Intermediate or "Objective 2" Area (not shown on page 49 map). The grant is 50% (maximum £25,000).

Again, application must be before the project commences.

The "Enterprise Initiative" includes many other initiatives to help small business in addition to the financial ones already mentioned above. Some of these other initiatives are:

Consultancy (This scheme ends in 1994). It provides consultancy assistance in a number of key business areas – marketing, design, quality, manufacturing and services systems, business planning and financial & management information systems. The help comes in two stages. First an Enterprise Counsellor will conduct a short free business review of the firm, which should highlight its strengths and weaknesses. The Counsellor will recommend how the Consultancy Initiatives can best help. Next the appropriate consultant will be brought in. The consultant will draw up terms of reference which can be agreed before any work commences.

The Government will pay one third of the cost of between 5 and 15 mandays of consultancy. In Assisted Areas (see page 49) and in Urban Programme Areas, the grant is one half of the cost. The firm has to pay the balance.

Innovation This initiative covers a wide range of assistance, including: consultancy, technology transfer and grants for research and development.

Other initiatives These include: Exporting, Managing into the '90s; Education & Training; Single European Market and Environment.

Enterprise Allowance This was an excellent national scheme (also known as the EAS) to help unemployed people who were trying to set up in business for themselves. The scheme still exists but is now managed locally and is known by different names. It provides

an allowance for unemployed people in the early stages of starting their own business.

The responsibility for managing this scheme rests with the Training and Enterprise Councils (TECs) in England & Wales and the Local Enterprise Companies (LECs) In Scotland.

In conclusion Government financial assistance can provide a vital source of funds for the new start business. However, with many schemes around, many applicable only to certain projects in certain areas, and all in a state of constant change it is imperative to seek expert advice from your local Enterprise Agency or other business development unit. But do not be too upset if there are no grants or subsidies for your particular project!

5. EQUITY FINANCIERS

(This only applies if you plan to set up a Limited Company).

Many people want to retain 100% control and ownership of their new business because they are convinced they will make their "millions" from it and they do not feel inclined to share the spoils. However, it takes a good deal of investment and business acumen to make one's fortune and those elusive millions are much more readily achievable if one is prepared to have a slice of a large cake rather than all of a small cake. There are two very good reasons for having an outside investor in your business – first, since an investor should contribute knowledge in addition to capital, choose your partners carefully and ask pointedly what they can offer by way of expertise, trade and customer contacts in addition to the money. Second, by having the money invested as equity (shares)

rather than loans you do not become "over-geared". Over-gearing is where the ratio of loans to share capital is such that the business's profits cannot support the interest payments on the loan and thus the business slowly sinks. Equity finance can come from one or indeed a combination of two main sources:

Private Investors In this case an individual invests directly in the business by purchasing shares. Shares are often a nominal £1 and so if the total capital being invested was £10,000 you may be investing £6,000 of your own (you will thereby own 60% of the company) while the other shareholder(s) invest the remaining £4,000. Thus there will be £10,000 of "issued share capital". If you did not want to give up as much of the equity or you wanted more funds, then this could be in the form of loans or by setting up more complicated financial structures. Note that an investor is better protected if some of his (or her) money is in the form of a loan, for if the business fails he (or she) is more likely to get some of the loan money back, whereas the share capital is likely to be lost.

Venture Capital This is for projects which are on the larger side of "small" with start-up capital in the £50,000 + category. Venture capitalists split into two entirely different sets of organisations with different motives. On the one hand there are the government development agencies who sometimes take an equity share in a new company if they see it to be a desirable business while on the other hand there are the private sector venture capitalists who are looking for a healthy return on their investment. Whereas the development agencies are prepared to make

... do not be too upset if there are no grants for your project!

investments as low as £10,000, the private sector venture capitalists are not normally interested in investments below the £50,000 mark (many have higher thresholds) though as usual there are exceptions. One important exception is *3i* (formerly Investors In Industry) which was formed in 1945 and is the largest company of its type in the field. They have offices in most major cities and their London office is at 91 Waterloo Road, London SE1 8XP. Tel: 071-928 3131.

A free government booklet "Finance Without Debt", which discusses venture capital, is available from TECs and LECs. There is also an HMSO publication "Directory of Sources of Venture Capital" available for £10.

The High Street Banks may also provide equity finance for larger projects.

Raising the Finance

Note that you usually have to pay fees for acquiring venture capital money. You may be charged "negotiation fees" (also called "commitment fees") for arranging the finance. This can vary from 2% to 7% which together with legal fees can reach 10% of the sum raised. In addition, some organisations also charge annual "management" fees.

An attractive point of equity finance is that companies, if empowered by their Articles of Association, can buy back their own shares out of capital provided certain safeguards are met. This mechanism may attract an outside investor as they can make a capital gain and recover their investment (assuming the business is successful) by selling back their shares to the company at a profit.

6. HP/LEASING FIRMS

Generally this is a more expensive way of raising finance than using a bank. However it can be useful for acquiring high value items such as vehicles or machinery if one has difficulty raising the required capital. Since the finance company usually retains ownership of the vehicle or equipment, they may be prepared to offer the finance even when your bank borrowing is on its limits. Obviously there is no point in a finance deal if you think you may have difficulty in meeting the repayments.

There are tax differences between Hire Purchase (HP) and Leasing which will require an accountant's advice. In any case get quotes from several HP or Leasing firms and read the small print carefully as their interest rates and conditions can vary markedly.

7. TRADE CREDIT

Another excellent source of finance is trade credit. This is where a supplier

*Venture Capitalists looking for ...
... a healthy return ...*

allows you time before you have to pay for the goods or services they have provided. A new business is often asked to pay up-front as it is an unknown credit risk, so if you can negotiate any credit period it will be a great help. Once you are trading, you may by negotiation stretch the normal 30 day period to 60 days or even longer. You should of course pay your bills by the agreed date. Failure to do so is not only poor business ethics but your supplier will note this and may either eventually remove your credit facility or simply be less accommodating on other matters.

Trade credit is also relevant if your customers are mainly trade as they will expect credit (even if you are a new

business). Credit control is vital to your cashflow. Issue your Invoices promptly and send out Statements at the end of the month (many companies pay only on Statements rather than Invoices) and follow up with phone calls if the payment date is passed. A suggestion to encourage their prompt payment is for you to offer a discount (2.5% is a typical figure) for payment made within 30 days.

8. OTHER SOURCES

Some business development agencies and local Enterprise Agencies have small sums of money (ie usually under £5,000 per project) for certain categories of applicants or projects in their area of operation.

For businesses that meet certain specific requirements, there are other very useful sources of start-up finance:

Prince's Youth Business Trust This scheme was the Prince of Wales own idea and he is its President. The Trust helps 18 to 29 year olds who are out of work and have some disadvantage (eg disabled or living in deprived areas) and who want to start up their own business, but are unable to raise the necessary finance.

The Trust can give grants up to £250 for market research, grants up to £1,500 for specific items such as tools and equipment and they can also give soft loans up to £5,000.

An important feature is that each business has their own adviser appointed to help them. The scheme is national with regional offices. Their headquarters are at 5 Cleveland Place, London SW1Y 6JJ. Tel: 071-321 6500.

Livewire Another initiative aimed at helping young people to start their own businesses, Livewire provides advice

for people aged 16 to 25 and awards cash prizes by their "Business Start Up Awards".

Livewire also operate their "Business Growth Challenge" programme where young owner managers spend a series of free residential weekends being given high quality management training to encourage further growth of their businesses.

Contact Livewire at Hawthorn House, Forth Banks, Newcastle-upon-Tyne NE1 3SG. Tel: 091-261 5584.

British Coal Enterprise Ltd They can provide soft loans and other assistance to any business planning to set up in a coal mining area. Tel: 0623 826833.

British Steel Industry Ltd This organisation helps businesses to start up, expand or relocate in 19 traditional steel areas around the country. They provide loans and/or share capital in amounts from £10,000 to £150,000. They can also provide work space for small businesses in some of the areas. Tel: 081-686 2311.

GOING, GOING . . . .

Enterprise Zones The zones can be quite small – often a specific industrial estate. Enterprise Zones last only 10 years and most have come to the end of their time. For those zones still within their 10-year lifetime (see list on page 49), advantages include exemption from rates and 100% tax allowances for capital expenditure on industrial and commercial buildings. Planning permission is also simplified and individual zones may have other incentives.

Business Expansion Scheme This was a complex government scheme to assist companies, but no new investment available after 1993. It has been replaced by the *Enterprise Investment Scheme.*

British Technology Group (BTG) The BTG no longer offers finance to companies who develop their own products, nor do they provide funds through their former industrial scheme.

KEY POINT Borrowed money has to be repaid! Ensure your Cashflow Forecast permits you to repay loans even if bank interest rates rise and your turnover drops.

KEY POINT Most new businesses start under-capitalised and this makes them vulnerable. It is therefore important that your Business Plan allows for contingencies. It is easier to raise money before a project commences than after several difficult months have elapsed■

Finding Premises

Your business will need premises even if it is just the front room of your home. The choice of premises is important and in certain cases such as a shop, restaurant or hotel, the decision can either make or break the business.

GENERAL POINTS

To Buy or Rent?   If you can afford it and if you are planning to remain at one location for several years it may be better to buy the property as it provides more security in the longer term. However, when you are starting a business, you probably do not want all your funds to be tied up in bricks and mortar, and so you will have little option but to rent. One exception is if you are taking over a small hotel or guest house when it is more usual to *buy*.

Location   Many people look for premises near to where they live. That could lead to them setting up in either a poor location or at best a marginal location. It is better to ask yourself "Where is the best place to set up my business?" The answer may be in an adjacent town or county!

Planning Permission   Check with the Planning Department of the local Council that the existing planning permission for the premises you are considering covers the activities you plan to perform. If not, you will need to apply for a "change of use". This can take a month or more. Classes of use include: residential, retail (several classes), offices, light industrial etc. One situation where planning permission can be a problem is if you want to sell directly to the public from a small factory as that is classed as "mixed use" (retail and industrial) and may not be acceptable to the local Council. If any structural alterations are required this will need Planning Permission. Additional problems occur with frontages and external signs in designated "conservation areas" so check that too.

Locating Premises   There is rarely one organisation that knows all the commercial properties to buy or rent in their area so you should do all of the following: a) contact your local Enterprise Agency or business development unit (especially for workshop and factory space), b) read the commercial property adverts in the local newspaper, c) visit estate agents who specialise in commercial property and also visit your Solicitors Property Centre. You could also insert an advert in the local newspaper under the "Premises Wanted" classification.

In the case of retail premises you should also walk the shopping streets looking for the "To Let" signs. The Enterprise Agency or business development unit will also be able to quote typical rental figures (usually given in terms of £/square foot/year) and typical rates payable. With the advent of the Uniform Business Rates, find out what implications this may have for you.

Always examine as many premises as possible to get the best property available. Don't just go for the first you see.

The Lease   If renting, this is the lengthy and detailed tenancy contract. It is an important document so read it carefully. It will cover − period of lease, rent, all responsibilities including those for insuring and repairing the premises (normally the tenant's responsibility), statutory liabilities, when rent reviews are due and the use and transferability of the lease (you want to be free to pass on the lease). Note that many leases permit the landlord to raise the rent by a fixed amount whenever a lease is reassigned. If the lease states you are responsible for the dilapidations, ie deterioration of the building during your tenancy, you should get a survey done and agreed with the landlord (it is also a good idea to take some photos!). Leases are not set in stone, so challenge hostile or unreasonable clauses and question any you do not understand. Find out if there is a Factor who is managing the property and what his charges are and if there are common charges. Always consult a solicitor regarding the lease, or if buying a property.

Surveyors   When you begin your search for premises another door you should knock on is that of a local chartered surveyor. He will advise you on suitable areas to look for premises, other areas to avoid, typical rents and so on. Once you have located premises (either to rent or buy) you would be advised to have the premises surveyed.

KEY POINT   Never sign a lease until you have completed your Business Plan, raised the finance, had the building surveyed and have discussed the lease terms with your own solicitor.

KEY POINT   When you take over any premises, remember to inform the local Authority (for Rates), British Telecom, Post Office, the Factor, and the Gas and Electricity offices (as appropriate) − and get meters read the day you move in.

SHOP PREMISES CHECKLIST

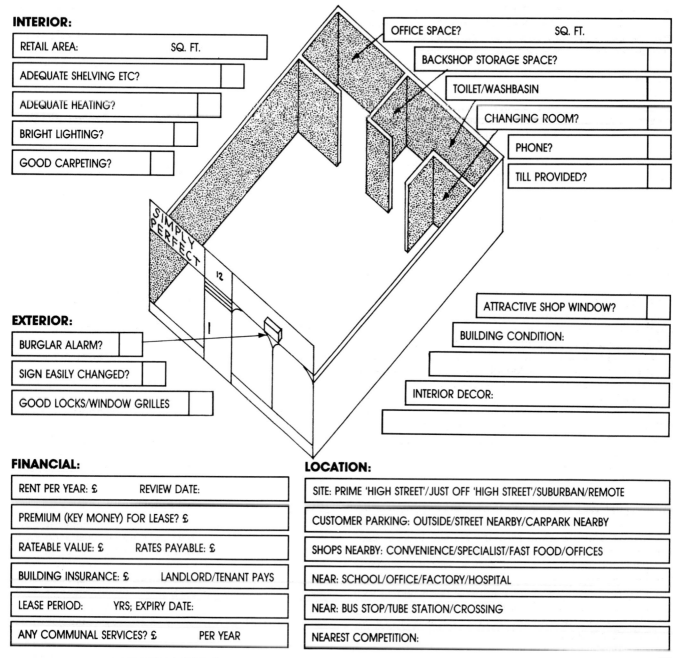

INTERIOR:

RETAIL AREA: SQ. FT.

ADEQUATE SHELVING ETC?

ADEQUATE HEATING?

BRIGHT LIGHTING?

GOOD CARPETING?

OFFICE SPACE?   SQ. FT.

BACKSHOP STORAGE SPACE?

TOILET/WASHBASIN

CHANGING ROOM?

PHONE?

TILL PROVIDED?

ATTRACTIVE SHOP WINDOW?

BUILDING CONDITION:

INTERIOR DECOR:

EXTERIOR:

BURGLAR ALARM?

SIGN EASILY CHANGED?

GOOD LOCKS/WINDOW GRILLES

FINANCIAL:

RENT PER YEAR: £   REVIEW DATE:

PREMIUM (KEY MONEY) FOR LEASE? £

RATEABLE VALUE: £   RATES PAYABLE: £

BUILDING INSURANCE: £   LANDLORD/TENANT PAYS

LEASE PERIOD: YRS; EXPIRY DATE:

ANY COMMUNAL SERVICES? £   PER YEAR

LOCATION:

SITE: PRIME 'HIGH STREET'/JUST OFF 'HIGH STREET'/SUBURBAN/REMOTE

CUSTOMER PARKING: OUTSIDE/STREET NEARBY/CARPARK NEARBY

SHOPS NEARBY: CONVENIENCE/SPECIALIST/FAST FOOD/OFFICES

NEAR: SCHOOL/OFFICE/FACTORY/HOSPITAL

NEAR: BUS STOP/TUBE STATION/CROSSING

NEAREST COMPETITION:

Finding Premises

DIFFERENT TYPES OF PREMISES

Working From Home   This is obviously the cheapest and simplest way for many businesses to start, and it is becoming popular, but there are legal constraints. In particular if you live in a rented or council-owned house it will almost certainly be a breach of your tenancy agreement to conduct any business from the house. Even if you own your home it may be an infringement of local planning regulations or bylaws to work from home and may also breach a condition of your ownership of the house. If you have a mortgage the Building Society may not like it either. If your neighbours object to your business activities, you could have a problem. So get legal advice and in addition ask your accountant about Capital Gains Tax and possible Business Rates implications.

However, the simple truth is that many businesses operate quite happily from homes (or domestic garages) maintaining a very low profile – minimal advertising (or only using a telephone number on adverts), no exterior signs, no noise, no queues of visiting customers or suppliers ... Be careful though about potential fire risks (such as welding) because you may discover, too late, that your domestic insurance does not cover you! If you live in a council-owned house a few discreet enquiries at the local government offices would let you know where you stand. With the exception of certain office-type activities or if the business is a service operation (such as painting & decorating) where the home is merely a base/office, working from home tends to be a short-term situation until a business gets established and moves into commercial premises.

Office   The main question to answer in this context is "Will customers need to visit the office and do they need to be impressed?" If you are dealing with large companies the answer may be yes but if not, you could opt for more modest premises. Again if people are expected to visit you is there adequate car parking and is the office near public transport for your customers? If your work requires a fair amount of movement of people between your office and your clients' offices it would obviously be wise to be located nearby. Be wary of upper floor offices with no lifts.

There are now office complexes where secretarial support (typing, reception, phone answering, fax, photocopying) is provided and this can be of great benefit to a small business not wanting to take on staff right away. In any office block be careful of your responsibilities for "common" repairs and any "joint management" charges

Many businesses operate happily from home ...
....maintaining a very low profile.

for security, cleaning etc both of which can be expensive. Finding suitable small office premises can be difficult. If the bulk of your work relates to one large company they may be happy to rent you a room in their own office block.

Shop   The 3 most important factors to consider when finding retail premises are: 1. Location, 2. Location and 3. Location! Remember too that the retail trade is changing – the chain stores have great financial strength; new shopping complexes are shifting the retail "centres" of towns, sometimes out of the town centres altogether; offices are encroaching on previously exclusive retail sites and shopping is becoming more of a family leisure activity. A street that was good for shopping in your childhood may now be a poor bet.

To assess a site, talk to people in the trade, talk to other shopkeepers nearby, take the advice of a local accountant and a local chartered surveyor. Visit the site at different times and different days of the week and count the passersby. Are they carrying shopping? Are they to be seen in the shops or just walking past? Check too that there is suitable parking and access so stock can be delivered easily. But most important of all, be careful not to be taken in by the cheery facade and glitter of retail sites.

WORKSHOP/SMALL FACTORY CHECKLIST ✓

FACILITIES:

WORKSHOP FLOOR AREA: SQ. FT.

LIGHTING: BULB/STRIP/NONE   QTY:

FLOOR SPACE CLEAR?

ROOF HEIGHT ADEQUATE?

HEATING: ELECT/GAS/CH/NONE

FLOOR: TIMBER/CONCRETE

EXTERIOR:

SIGN USABLE?

SERVICE DOOR ADEQUATE?

GOOD LOCKS/WINDOW GRILLES

BURGLAR ALARM/WATCHMAN

FINANCIAL:

RENT PER YEAR: £   REVIEW DATE:

RENT FREE CONCESSIONS?   HOW LONG?

RATEABLE VALUE: £   RATES PAYABLE: £   CONCESSIONS?

BUILDING INSURANCE: £   LANDLORD/TENANT PAYS

LEASE PERIOD: YRS;   EXPIRY DATE: NOTICE PERIOD:

ANY COMMUNAL SERVICES?   £   PER YEAR

BUILDING CONDITION:

INTERIOR DECOR:

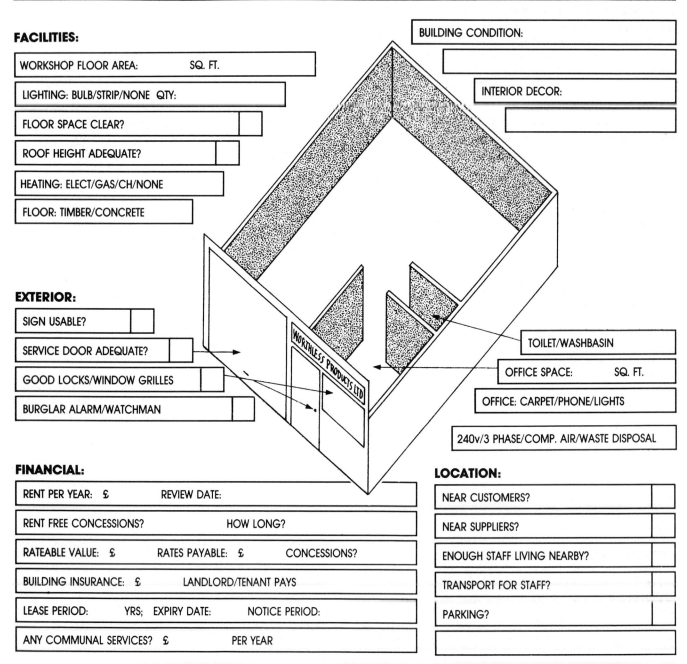

TOILET/WASHBASIN

OFFICE SPACE: SQ. FT.

OFFICE: CARPET/PHONE/LIGHTS

240v/3 PHASE/COMP. AIR/WASTE DISPOSAL

LOCATION:

NEAR CUSTOMERS?

NEAR SUPPLIERS?

ENOUGH STAFF LIVING NEARBY?

TRANSPORT FOR STAFF?

PARKING?

Finding Premises

Check too with an insurance broker as certain areas (and certain types of stock) may be regarded as high risk from a security point-of-view and this could make your contents insurance expensive. The insurance companies might also insist on a burglar alarm which is an additional expense.

The demand for good shop sites is such that you may have to pay a "premium" (also called "key money") for the benefit of taking over a lease. This is a once-off payment for the privilege of taking over a desirable lease and it can be expensive. If the rent was set several years before and the next rent review is not due for a couple of years, then the incoming tenant *may* get the lease at the existing rent which could be lower than the going market rate. In that case, this benefit to the incoming tenant is often reflected in the premium he has to pay.

If your proposed shop is to stock food consult the Environmental Health Department of your local authority to ascertain what regulations are in force. Converting non-food premises for food may be very costly. The choice of location for a shop is closely related to your market research results — see the chapter **Doing The Market Research**. See also the Checklist on page 55.

Workshop/Small Factory   There are new, old and refurbished units available almost everywhere but in certain areas of the country there will be a shortage of the most popular units (ie under 1,000 square feet). There are both private sector and government landlords (either local councils or development agencies). You *may* be able to extract more concessions from the latter but do not expect to pay much less than the privately owned units. The golden rule is to take on the smallest premises you can get by with but ensure your lease allows you to transfer to a larger unit, if required, without attracting financial penalties. Older premises tend to be cheaper though rents fluctuate widely depending upon the type of building and size, but can be higher for small custom-built "nursery" units.

If you are hoping to sell direct to the public from the unit or work on cars you may face problems with planning permission. In contrast, manufacturing businesses are considered particularly desirable by the government development agencies and various concessions may be negotiated such as rent free periods, reduced rates and so on. Remember that such "carrots" end so allow for this in your forward cashflow projections. Remember also to contact your local Health & Safety Executive officer (see the Phone Book) to find out what regulations are relevant to your proposed business. See also the Checklist on page 57.

Café/Restaurant/Bar   As with shops, location is crucial. Whereas a "fast-food" outlet or café requires a prime high street location a good restaurant or bar can afford to be elsewhere, but not just anywhere! Depending upon the clientele parking could also be essential. Check with the local Environmental Health Department for information on regulations and check too with the Fire Officer. If you plan to sell alcohol check on local licensing laws and opening hours. If the premises are not currently used for the same purpose then Planning Permission may be a problem.

Small Hotel/Guest House   To find the correct location for a hotel one must know *precisely* the clientele who would use the hotel. For instance, if it is mainly overnight Bed & Breakfast people then one needs to be in a highly visible location on a road carrying suitable traffic. In contrast, if it is mainly longer-stay tourists, one needs to be located where tourists go — contact your local Tourist Board to find out who comes, from where, at what times of the year, what accommodation they look for and whether the total numbers are rising or falling. If the clientele are mainly business people what accommodation do they require?

Before you either take over an existing hotel or convert a building to a hotel a great deal of market research must be done as once you buy you are heavily committed. Beware of buildings of "special architectural merit" especially if they are termed "listed buildings" as insurance cover could be extremely high and general repair work can be equally costly as it may be necessary to reinstate, for instance, ornate stonework.

If you own your own home you may consider selling it and putting the money towards the purchase of the hotel.

If you are going to serve food, you must contact your local Environmental Health Department at a very early stage as there are stringent regulations.

Note that if the hotel sleeps more than 6 people (including staff or guests) or if some sleeping accommodation is on any floor above the first floor or in the basement then it must have a Fire Certificate. You should also check on other local licensing requirements.

Adverts and estate agents are the best sources to find places to buy, and always have a full structural survey carried out before signing anything■

STARTING

Chapters

Designing Letterheads Etc

The design of letterheads and business cards are not normally given enough consideration. They are after all an advert for your firm. When you send out a letter to a prospective customer it creates an instant impression of your business standards in terms of quality, professionalism and style. Often your letter will be you introducing your service to a new customer or it may be a quotation for a contract. In both cases you are trying to sell your business on the strength of what is on that small piece of paper — so it really is quite important.

Some business stationery uses striking colours, some use interesting artistic effects or graphic designs but even if yours is quite simple and produced on a low budget it is important that it is well laid out and smart. You will probably need the help of a professional designer or printer who will know how to get the best effect from a one colour print, an imaginative layout and well-considered choice of lettering.

Before doing anything some decisions have to be made:

Business Name In the chapter **Making It Legal** mention was made of trading under a business name rather than your own name. There are certain firms, such as solicitors, accountants and consultants, who traditionally trade under the names of the partners. Otherwise the opportunity of trading under a business name should not be missed. A business name should convey a sales message to your customers and is therefore a cheap yet powerful promotional tool. Some hints for choosing a business name are:

1. Pretend you are standing in your customer's shoes. What is it about your business that makes him or her choose *you?* Is it your speed, good service, wide choice of products, convenience, specialised service ... whatever it is, your name should reflect it.

2. Keep the name short. The "London Stainless Steel Flanged Bolts Co Ltd" may be a highly descriptive title but is obviously too long and will pose a problem should they diversify into brass!

3. Choose a word or words which roll off the tongue and are easy to say.

4. Check your local Phone Book to ensure no-one else has a similar business name. (If you are forming a limited company the company registration agent must check to ensure your proposed name is unique).

Company Logo A logo is a symbol by which you hope customers will identify you and your products. We are all familiar with logos and it can be an important promotional tool but it takes a long time and plenty of promotion before people learn to recognise it. Because of this it is not so useful when starting a small business, but if you have a good idea for a logo use it if you can.

Corporate Image Related to logos but of more relevance to a small company is to have a standardised corporate image. By this we mean standardised colour(s), graphics and typefaces which you use on everything related to the business — letterheads, business cards, invoices, products, packaging, promotional literature, advertisements, van sides, interior decor and even staff uniforms.

DESIGN ASPECTS

Colour Your business may be associated with something that people naturally identify with a given colour. Examples are: agriculture (green); aircraft/airlines (sky blue); shipping/marine (navy blue or grey); military (drab olive); sunshine (yellow) and so on. The primary colours (red, blue, yellow) tend to be associated with bold things, probably with a young image. In contrast, two-tone dark/light grey and brown/cream are more sophisticated. Gold and silver have appropriate connotations of wealth. Maroon, damson and violet are rich, possibly evening-related colours.

Before you get carried away remember that with anything you print each colour almost doubles the price and black printing is cheaper than any other colour. Remember too that if you choose a light colour (especially light blue) you will have difficulty making photocopies, if that is relevant.

Typefaces The different styles of lettering are known as typefaces and there are literally hundreds to choose from! Some commonly used typefaces are Univers, Helvetica (which is not unlike Univers) and Times Roman. These are also usually available in **bold** or *italic* forms. All lettering can be printed in different sizes, called the "point size". This book is set in 10 point, while this text is in 9 point and this text is in 11 point. A typeface just like a business name or colour conveys a message to the reader. For instance, the typeface called **STENCIL** looks rather military or related to packing cases (maybe an import/export business); an elaborate typeface such as *Script* looks rather dignified while 𝔒𝔩𝔡 𝔈𝔫𝔤𝔩𝔦𝔰𝔥 speaks for itself.

The Quick Guide to Letterheads

For a **Sole Trader** or **Partnership**, the example left shows the three legal requirements for a letterhead: a) business name, b) UK business address and c) the name of the sole trader (or partners). Several other optional features are shown ie a sales message, fold line and dots for window envelope. For full details, see page right.

SIMPLY PERFECT

12 Regent Crescent
Greenock
PA1 1ZZ

Tel: Greenock (0475) 242

The shop for ladies who dress to perfection
Proprietor: Joan Smith

Worthless Products Ltd

Unit 3
Industrial Estate
Birmingham B1 1ZZ
Tel: 021-123 456
Fax: 021-123 789

Manufacturers of Novelty Goods

Registered in England No. 0000
Registered Office: Unit 3, Industrial Estate, Birmingham B1 1ZZ

For a **Limited Company**, the example right shows the four legal requirements for a letterhead: a) full company name with Limited or Ltd, b) country of registration, c) registered number and d) the registered office address. Note that if you choose to add the Directors' names, then all names must be given. For full details see page right.

Due to space limitations, we have not tried to show a clever design of letterhead or the use of logos etc.

Designing Letterheads Etc

DESIGNING A LETTERHEAD

This is assuming of course that your business venture actually needs a letterhead, if not, ignore this section. Designing the letterhead involves choosing:

Paper Size   A4 (210 x 297mm) is becoming fairly standard in the UK. It fits most envelopes, files and photocopiers.

Paper Type   Letterheads are usually done on white paper. Coloured paper can be effective but has several disadvantages − it needs matching envelopes and second sheets, may photocopy poorly and it could be difficult to correct typing errors. The weight of paper is usually 75 or 100 grams/square metre but if you really want to impress, you can use the more expensive cartridge paper.

Typeface (ie Lettering)   See notes above. You may choose a fancy typeface for the business name and a plainer typeface, such as Univers, for the address etc. You can also get the lettering done by thermography which raises it slightly and looks effective but costs more.

Colour   Black is the cheapest colour to use for printing. All other standard colours are about the same price. Printing in two colours (black is also a "colour"), costs nearly double. With a single colour, additional effects can be achieved by using reverse text or "screening" which gives a lighter shade of colour. If you are trying to project a young and trendy image gaudy colours may be fine, but remember that they might be inappropriate for, say, a sober engineering company.

Phone/Fax Details   An increasing amount of business is done over the phone. Here are several suggestions for a letterhead: a) if the number consists of a town name followed by the number, eg Oxford 316, then include the dialling code in brackets, eg Oxford (0865) 316, b) if you have a telephone answering machine connected it may be useful to note this because it warns the caller that they may find themselves speaking to a machine and it also indicates that a message can be left at any time and c) you may consider giving a home phone number in addition to an office number if you expect important calls outwith normal office hours. If you have a fax or telex machine then you should also add those numbers on the letterhead.

Sales Message   Your letter may be going to potential customers and it is therefore an excellent medium to carry a short sales message. Typical messages could be: a) names of companies you represent (if likely to be known to the reader), written along the top or bottom of the letterhead, b) the products or services your company provides or c) a message such as "We import the finest silks" or "Your problems are our problems" or whatever!

Other Information   Pre-printed words such as "Date:...", "Your Ref:...", "Our Ref:...", "File Ref:..." are becoming less fashionable and should only be added if you feel your own administration needs it.

Some Letterhead Legalities

For a sole trader or partnership the letterhead must, by law, include the following information: a) business name (if used), b) business address in Great Britain (include the post code) and c) names of the sole trader or all partners.

For a limited company, the letterhead must, by law, include the following information: a) full company name (including "Ltd" or "Limited"), b) the country of registration (England, Scotland, Ireland or Wales), c) the registered number, ie "Registered in England No: *****" and d) its registered office address. If the letterhead is to show the Directors' names then every Director's name must be shown.

Layout

There are many acceptable styles of layout, but here are some tips:

1. Do not use print that is too small to read easily or a layout that forces the reader to search for your name, phone number etc.

2. It is usual to place your address block at the top of the letterhead with the business name either just above the address or placed centrally.

3. Put Proprietor(s) names at the foot of the letter.

4. Most envelopes require an A4 letterhead to be folded in three − a small printed "fold" line (about 5mm long) at the appropriate place at the left edge of the paper can make life easier.

5. If you use "window" envelopes, mark the window area on the letterhead with tiny corner dots − this helps the typist. (Note: window envelopes save lots of time).

Designing Letterheads Etc

DESIGNING A BUSINESS CARD

A business card is useful whenever your business is such that you would normally know the name of your customer and he or she would know your name. It is therefore a very personal communication. It is almost essential if you are dealing with trade customers or government agencies. First, some basic design decisions need to be made:

Card Size   Many business people "file" the cards they receive in wallets or holders specially designed for the purpose. It is sensible therefore to keep your card to the standard size (ie about 9 x 5½cm) so that it will fit these holders. Another point is that business cards that open like greetings cards may not fit into these wallets or holders mentioned above.

Card Type   A thin floppy business card feels cheap and conveys a poor image.

Typeface And Colour   These should mimic the letterhead to get a standardised "corporate image".

Layout   There is much more freedom here than with a letterhead and scope for some interesting graphic design work. The most important aspect is to keep the name and job title clear and prominent. If more than one person in your business needs a business card, each card should be identical except for changing the name and job title.

The Information to be Printed on the Card

A business card carries different information to a letterhead for whereas a letterhead is issued by the *firm*, the business card is issued by an *individual* of that firm. So pride of place on the card should be given to the card user's name and position in the firm (ie your job title).

Name   Following American practice the business world seems to be dropping "Mr, Mrs, Miss or Ms" and using first names more. If you are selling *expertise* you could include any qualifications you have after your name.

Job Title   Your title is important as it conveys your status and area of responsibility. If there are two partners you could say "Partner" but it would be better to reflect the role they play, eg "Sales Manager" and for a limited company: "Sales Director", "Production Director" etc.

Firm's Name & Address   This should be complete with post code and phone/fax numbers. If dealing with overseas companies, do include "United Kingdom".

Sales Message   If space permits it is useful to put a sales message on your card, even if this is merely a brief statement as to what your firm does. Sales leaflets and brochures get misplaced and lost but people tend to hold on to business cards. If you are offering a service that a client will only require on occasions it is particularly important to word the message carefully as it could close a sale.

Reverse Side   Some people use this for their home address and phone number or a more extended sales message. It will cost more to print on both sides of the card and remember that in many business card wallets the reverse side gets covered by another card. Also, leaving the reverse blank can be useful for handwritten notes, off-the-cuff quotations etc.

OTHER STATIONERY

To save on printing costs for invoices, receipts and statements you can use a letterhead with the appropriate word, eg "INVOICE", typed as a heading (this practice is useful where the sums of money are large and you are not raising such invoices frequently). An alternative is to buy a rubber stamp (or small pre-printed labels) with your name and address (and VAT number if registered) and use one of the pre-printed duplicate books which are available from most stationers ■

Employing Staff

Almost all businesses need to employ staff as they grow. Some of these people are excellent and an essential and valuable part of the firm but think very hard before you take on any staff.

Employing anyone is very expensive — in addition to paying their wages when they are working, you have to pay them when they are on holiday or sick for a day or when they need an afternoon off to visit the dentist, and so on. Also, there is a tax on employment — it is called the Employers National Insurance contribution and it currently exceeds 10% of wages for all higher paid staff. Finally, the paperwork and mandatory returns associated with employing staff is onerous and to cap it all staff can let you down badly. Keep in mind the golden rules:

* Take on staff only if you *have* to.

* Beware of recruiting in *anticipation* of demand.

* Interview carefully.

* Get rid of bad employees as fast as legally possible.

* Encourage, train, reward and keep good employees.

WHY EMPLOY STAFF?

Perhaps you do not need to actually employ staff at all or at least not yet. Here are some typical situations and possible solutions that save you from taking on more staff:

1. Telephone Answering You may think you need someone to answer the phone but an answering machine may be all you require or (in most cities) there are agencies that will take your calls for you for a fee. Or you may use a portable phone if you are out and about a lot.

Perhaps you need some help?

2. Typing Letters You may be unable to type, but you may have a spouse, relative or friend who is prepared to type the odd letter for a nominal fee.

3. Office Work You may have a rush of office work — so why not use a "temp" from a secretarial agency?

4. Book-keeping All businesses need someone to keep the accounts books and if you do not want to yourself, then there are freelance book-keepers who will do the books for you.

5. Deliveries You may need someone to drive a van to deliver your products or collect materials, so why not use one of the many parcel services?

6. Selling You may need someone to go out and get orders. There are now organisations who simply market other people's products and services. Alternatively you could use an agent and pay them commission — but if you are thinking of this take advice for it can be frustrating and unrewarding.

7. Manufacturing/Assembly Many sectors of our manufacturing industry are running at under-capacity so why not sub-contract your manufacturing or assembly work? This can apply to heavy, light and electronics engineering. Another way of sub-contracting is to use "cottage workers" (also called "outworkers") — this is where people work at home as if self-employed and it is used particularly for knitwear, garments and for "stuffing" electronic printed circuit boards. One note of caution — many "outworkers" are now deemed to be employees under employment law, so first take advice.

RECRUITING STAFF

There are 5 basic ways to find staff:

1. Word-of-Mouth This can be useful as the applicant may already be known to someone whom you know and trust. Once you get started ask your existing staff.

2. Card In Window For some low qualification jobs, one may advertise by putting a postcard in the window of the local newsagent.

3. Jobcentre These can be very useful and may, if required, do initial interviewing for you.

4. Newspaper Adverts This is obviously more expensive but casts your net wider. Choose a newspaper that your potential applicant is likely to read. For specialised jobs an advert in a trade or professional magazine may be more appropriate. Before you advertise

Employing Staff

check several copies of the publication to see if there are similar adverts from other firms and what wages they are offering. Your advert should describe the job adequately giving the wage offered and the likely age band and experience/qualifications of the applicant you are seeking. Try not to use Box Numbers if they can be avoided as this can be off-putting to some people. Be careful about what you say — it can be contractually binding and avoid the phrase "permanent employment".

5. Recruitment Agencies. These are expensive as they charge for the adverts they place plus a fee equivalent to 10% (or more) of the annual salary of the recruit. The main advantages of using an agency are they often have a number of suitable people on their books and they will do the initial interviewing of applicants.

Application Form When applicants contact you, either send them or give them an Application Form to complete. See the example opposite. (Note that to save space in this book, the form has been condensed in size to one page — normally it would require both sides of an A4 sheet. You could type out the form then take photocopies to issue).

It is a good idea for Application Forms to be completed in hand-writing as any job involves some written communication and if the applicant's writing is barely decipherable it is best to know at this stage. It also reveals the attention to detail and care of the applicant — a messy Application Form is likely to come from a careless person!

Application Forms of unsuccessful candidates should be kept for 6 months or more in case of any complaints of racial/sexual discrimination.

For candidates you take on you should keep the forms until some time after they leave your employment.

INTERVIEWING

An interview has two objectives — it allows the applicant to assess your firm and it allows you to assess the applicant. You need somewhere comfortable and quiet to conduct the interview, eg your business premises at the end of the working day (to prevent interruptions) or you could use a small "private function" room at a nearby hotel. Make certain the applicants know where and when the interview is to take place. If you are interviewing several people one after another you need a second person (eg the Receptionist if using a hotel) to handle the new arrivals, and a separate waiting room for them. Allow at least an hour for each interview — much longer for key managerial jobs.

One common error when interviewing is our natural instinct to size up people in an instant by their physical attractiveness, dress and manner of speech. Try hard not to form an opinion until the end of the interview!

There is also the risk that candidates with physical characteristics or interests similar to the interviewer will be looked on too favourably.

Remember that not only is the applicant trying to "sell" himself or herself to your firm, but you also need to "sell" your firm as it is important to attract a good applicant to join.

Warning: A contract need not be in writing so if you make verbal promises during the interview they could be legally binding.

Competence Tests It is very important to check the skills of applicants.

They may claim lots of qualifications and/or experience but a few simple tests can prove revealing. For instance, if interviewing a potential secretary, ask them to type a letter and take dictation. Or when interviewing junior electronics technicians you could start by asking them to identify components on a printed circuit board and then ask them the function of these components. For a manual skill such as metalwork, joinery, welding etc set practical tests. In all cases these competence tests should be similar to what they would have to do in the job.

Where the competence is more intellectual than manual, another technique is to get the applicant to join you for a day when you are doing what the applicant would have to do if he or she got the job. For instance if you were recruiting a Sales Manager then by visiting customers with the applicant

---

Some Interview Tips...

Do put the applicant at ease
Do offer them a coffee
Do sit at a similar height
Do get the applicant talking
Do ask open-ended questions
Do take notes

Don't be influenced by first impressions
Don't sit behind a desk
Don't sit with a bright light behind you
Don't avoid awkward or embarassing questions
Don't forget to talk about pay, holidays etc

Employing Staff – Application Form

Position Applied For: ....

Please answer ALL questions, in INK, in your own hand-writing. Where there is an asterisk (*), please delete as necessary.

Personal Details

Full Name: Mr/Mrs/Miss/Ms* ....

Date Of Birth: .... 19........ Country Of Birth: .... Nationality: ....

Present Address: .... Postcode: ....

Tel No (During Day): .... Nat. Ins. No: ..../......./......./......./.......

Single/Married/Divorced/Separated*   UK Driving Licence No: ....

No. and ages of dependent children: ....

Details of any serious accident/illness/disability: ....

....

Person to be contacted in emergency. Name: ....

Address: .... Tel No: ....

Educational Qualifications

Membership of any professional organisation/institution: .... Foreign languages: ....

Date (eg 6/86) From | To	Names of all secondary schools, colleges and universities attended	For schools — exams passed and grade For colleges/university — course and qualifications (Note any prizes, scholarships etc)
	Extend as necessary	

Work Experience (Including temporary and part-time jobs and service in HM Forces)

Date (eg 6/86) From | To	Name and address of employer	Position held with details of duties	Salary on leaving £	Reason for leaving
	Extend as necessary			

General

What notice required by present employer: .... Interests and hobbies: ....

Offices or other positions attained in any club or sport: ....

Declaration

I declare that to the best of my knowledge and belief the particulars on this application form are correct.

Signed: .... Date: ....

Employing Staff – Interview Questionnaire

(Make additional notes on reverse of form) (* Delete as necessary)

Applicants Name ....

Application Form
(Go through the form requesting clarification of any point).
Additional questions:

1. Do you smoke? Yes/No*   2. When did you move to present address? ....

3. Is the house — your own/rented privately/council/live with others*?

4. (If married) Does your husband/wife work?   Yes/No* Where? ....

5. (If spouse works and there are young children) Who looks after your children during the day? ....

6. Are you in good health?   Yes/No* How many days were you off work last year? ....

7. Driving Licence? Yes/No* Had any accidents or convictions? Yes/No*

8. Do you own a car? Yes/No*   Type ....   Regn. No. ....

9. Name, title and address of 2 work references plus bank (list overpage)?

10. Are you prepared to work overtime/additional hours? Yes/No*

Competence Tests

Details of tests set ....

Results ....

Statement of Employment
(The following forms the basis of information for the Job Offer letter.)

1. Job Title ....   2. Job Start Date .... 19............

3. Salary £.../hr, day, week, month*   4. Other bonuses/overtime ....
   (Paid by cash, cheque, credit transfer*)

5. Normal hours of work ....   Days ....

6. Holidays .... days/weeks* per year plus national holidays

7. Sick pay provision discussed? Yes/No*   8. Pension scheme discussed? Yes/No*

9. Period of written notice required by both parties ....

10. Disciplinary rules discussed? Yes/No*

11. Grievance procedure discussed? Yes/No*

Interview Expenses

Amount Paid £ ....   for ....

Interviewers signature ....   Date .... 19............

you would get some idea of how he or she operated under real conditions.

References Always check up on the references given. Often you get more information by phoning rather than writing to the referees. References from previous employers are very important as you want to know how the applicant performs at work. It is also relevant to know why they left their previous employers. Where an employee is likely to handle cash, a good idea is to ask for the applicant's bank as one reference (you will need to write to them as they are unlikely to answer a verbal request). Private character references from eg a vicar should be viewed in the light that they have been selected by the applicant to show them in a favourable light.

Job Offer Letter Once you have found a suitable person and checked their references then you may wish to send them a letter offering them the job. It is a legal requirement to provide, in writing, the terms of employment for every employee who works 16 hours or more per week (note: after 5 years continuous service this drops to 8 hours per week), and this statement has to be provided within 13 weeks of joining. Since the statement has to cover topics that should have been discussed at the interview the job offer letter and legally required statement could be combined — see the fictitious example later in this chapter. It must be pointed out that employment legislation has become very complex and you would be wise to get your solicitor to check your own Job Offer letter.

If the references have not yet been checked or the applicant has to have a medical examination, the letter could state "this offer is conditional on satisfactory references (or medical report) being received". If you state the job offer is for a "trial" or "probationary" period then be sure to add that this can be terminated by statutory notice thus avoiding any possibility of a fixed term contract.

One suggestion is to attach a copy of the job offer letter with wording such as the following typed at the foot, "Signed as acceptance of the above offer and conditions" together with "Date" and "Please Return In Enclosed Envelope". This makes it easier for candidates as all they have to do is read the job offer letter and if they agree, they sign and return the copy, retaining the original.

It is good manners to write to all unsuccessful applicants but it is most unwise to explain why he or she has been rejected as that may give them cause to sue you on discriminatory grounds. So keep it polite but short.

EMPLOYMENT LEGISLATION

Please note this section is for general guidance only and should not be regarded as a complete or authoritative statement of the law.

Payslip Each employee is entitled to be given a payslip with their wage packet or pay cheque. The payslip should itemise: gross pay, deductions (eg National Insurance, PAYE), variables (eg overtime, bonuses) and net pay. Where there are deductions the amount, interval and purpose should be noted.

Unfair Dismissal Before dismissing anyone, do take professional advice. It is a tricky legal area. Grounds for dismissal include incompetence, misconduct or redundancy, but must be "fair and reasonable". An employee cannot normally claim unfair dismissal until he/she has worked for you for 2 years. After one month's continuous service, an employee is entitled to a period of notice (or payment-in-lieu). Up to 2 years the minimum period of notice is one week but after 2 years this period of notice is increased by one week for every year of continuous employment up to a maximum of 12 weeks for 12 or more years service.

After 2 years, a dismissed employee is entitled, at their request, to receive a letter explaining why they are being dismissed.

Unless the employee is found guilty of a serious offence such as stealing or assault, it would be good management practice to allow the employee adequate opportunity to change his or her ways — they should have had at least one written warning, and possibly two, which should spell out: a) what they are doing wrong, b) what they must do to correct that and c) the consequences should they ignore the warnings. The second or "final written warning" as it is usually called should clearly state that no improvement/repetition will lead to dismissal. In addition you should have fully and fairly investigated the situation and allowed the employee to have his or her "say".

Where dismissal is in breach of contract, it is more likely to be a case of "wrongful dismissal".

Sex Discrimination Act and Equal Pay Act Remember that women have equal job opportunities to men and must be paid the same rate for the same job or for work of a broadly similar nature or equal value.

Worthless Products Ltd

Fictitious example

**Unit 3
Industrial Estate
Birmingham B1 1ZZ
Tel: 021-123 456**

Miss C.A. Jones
635, Unlikely Avenue
Birmingham

26th September 1985

Dear Miss Jones

Thank you for coming to the interview recently. We would like to offer you the position of <u>Machine Operator</u>, commencing 0900hrs, Monday 14th October 1985.

Your duties will be the operation of the Widget Mk3 Machine and any other associated equipment and general assistance with the assembly of our products. You will be expected to undertake reasonable alternative duties at the request of management. You will be responsible to Mr Brown – the Production Manager. Your Main Terms and Conditions of Employment are as follows:

<u>Pay:</u> Your pay will be £.. per hour, paid weekly in arrears by cheque.

<u>Overtime:</u> This is paid at a rate of .. once your normal daily basic hours have been worked.

<u>Hours of Work:</u> Normal hours of work are Monday to Friday, 0830 to 1700hrs with one hour for lunch, which is usually 1200 to 1300hrs.

<u>Holidays:</u> You will be entitled to 3 weeks paid holiday per year plus national holidays.

<u>Sickness:</u> If you are sick you must notify the office within an hour of your normal starting time. For illness lasting 7 days or more a Doctor's certificate is required. Statutory Sick Pay (SSP) will be paid from your fourth day of sickness. Any payments above SSP will be at the discretion of management.

<u>Pension:</u> There is at present no company pension scheme. A contracting-out certificate under the Social Security Pensions Act 1975 is not in force for this employment.

<u>Discipline & Grievances:</u> The disciplinary rules which apply to you can be found in the Company Handbook a copy of which is enclosed. If you are dissatisfied with any disciplinary decision or wish to seek redress of any grievance relating to your job you should write to the Production Manager. Further steps following such an application are outlined in the Handbook.

<u>Notice:</u> You will be required to give the company one week's written notice to terminate your employment. You are entitled to receive the following periods of notice from the company: over 1 month but under 2 years service - 1 week; over 2 years service - 1 week for each complete year of service to a maximum of 12 weeks notice after 12 years service.

Please confirm by returning the copy letter with your acceptance and signature on it as soon as possible. If you have any queries please contact me. We look forward to you working here and hope you will find it rewarding and enjoyable.

Yours sincerely

John Smith

John Smith
Administration Manager

Registered in England No. 0000
Registered Office: Unit 3, Industrial Estate, Birmingham B1 1ZZ

Manufacturers of Novelty Goods

Employing Staff

Health and Safety At Work This applies to employers, employees and the self-employed. If employing staff you should either give them each a copy of the leaflet "Health and Safety Law – What you should know", or display the poster. Every firm employing 5 or more people must, by law, write down its policy for their health and safety. If you are a manufacturer you should contact the Health and Safety Executive at an early stage to establish what regulations are appropriate.

Trade Unions If a trade union contacts you wishing to meet you to discuss various matters, take professional advice before you even agree to meet, for dealing with the union may be deemed as recognition of that union – and that has many implications of which you should be fully aware.

Statutory Sick Pay (SSP) This pays sickness benefit for most employees for a set period of time. If an employee is sick for 4 or more consecutive days (including weekends) then you can pay them SSP at fixed rates. Full details are given in your PAYE "New Employers Starter Pack" referred to in the chapter **Making it Legal**.

Maternity A woman employee has certain rights if she becomes pregnant. See the Department of Employment booklet PL 710 entitled "Employment rights for the expectant mother".

Confidentiality If your work involves trade secrets you may be able to get your employees to sign a non-disclosure agreement. This is best included as a clause in the terms of employment statement. Such a clause can prevent them from passing on information about your secret processes and the names of your customers. It can also prevent them competing directly against you but it cannot prevent them using their technical skill or trade knowledge to earn a living. This is a tricky area of law so requires expert professional advice.

Giving Notice After one month's continuous employment a full-time employee is entitled to a minimum of 1 week's notice. From 2 years they are entitled to 1 week per complete year of service up to a maximum of 12 weeks.

Guarantee Payments If you plan to temporarily lay-off staff due to a shortage of work, first read the Department of Employment's booklet PL 724 on "Guarantee Payments".

Redundancy This occurs when a firm wants to reduce its staff. The Department of Employment must be given at least 30 days notice if you plan to make more than 10 people redundant. Redundancy is only relevant if the employee concerned has been with you continuously for 2 years or more. Redundancy payments are calculated as follows: for each year of employment in which the employee was age 18 to 21 – ½ weeks wage/year of employment; from age 22 to 40 – 1 weeks wage/year of employment; age 41 plus – 1½ weeks wage/year of employment over age 41. Entitlement is to a maximum of 20 years and there is a maximum weekly value.

Transfer of Undertakings If planning to buy or sell an existing business, note the Transfer of Undertakings (Protection of Employment) Regulations protects employee's jobs when a business is taken over.

GETTING HELP

For advice on most aspects of employment legislation, contact the nearest offices of ACAS (the Advisory, Conciliation and Arbitration Service). They have offices in Accrington, Birmingham, Bristol, Cardiff, Fleet, Glasgow, Leeds, Liverpool, London, Manchester, Newcastle and Nottingham.

If you want advice about how to operate National Insurance, SSP or Statutory Maternity Pay, phone the DSS on: 0800 393539. The call is free.

A GENERAL COMMENT . . . .

Employing staff can present particular problems for a new small business. For instance, it can be difficult attracting high-calibre people to join a fledgling enterprise; unskilled or junior staff require a great deal of supervision and the paperwork related to employing staff is time-consuming. Finally, some proprietors have difficulty in accepting that their employees are likely to be less dedicated than themselves■

FOOTNOTE

Wages Councils The Wages Councils used to fix the minimum hourly rates and overtime for workers over 21 in many trades, but the Councils are in the process of being abolished.

Doing Basic Officework

You may well loathe doing "paperwork" but it *really is* an essential part of every business venture, so here are some ideas on how to do it simply and effectively. There is also great satisfaction to be had from being organised and up-to-date with your paperwork.

OFFICE EQUIPMENT

You do not really need a new desk, executive high back chair or similar paraphernalia but what you may require is:

(1) a telephone; (2) a table used exclusively for your paperwork; (3) a comfortable chair to use at the table; (4) a filing cabinet (purchased second-hand if possible, and consider too if it should be fireproof); (5) a small electric typewriter; (6) several clean cardboard boxes (approx 12″ by 12″) to temporarily "file" papers; (7) lots of blank A4 paper and other stationery items such as a stapler, paper clips, hole punch, ball pens etc and finally, (8) a cheap "IN" tray, "PENDING" tray and "OUT" tray for your table.

Always keep these costs down when starting a new business as they do not make profits!

...... cardboard boxes to temporarily "file" papers.

Desirable equipment includes computers, photocopiers and fax machines. Computers are discussed in the later chapter **Using A Computer**. In the case of photocopiers only consider getting one if your business involves a significant amount of paperwork. If possible, use instead an instant photocopy shop. If you need to send documents or letters quickly, especially if dealing with overseas customers or suppliers, then a fax machine may be very useful.

LETTERS

Handling incoming mail requires a certain amount of discipline. Whenever mail arrives always put it in the "IN" tray on your desk even before you open it, or place the mail in some other fixed location where it will not be mislaid. When you sit down to tackle the mail try to handle each letter or document once only ie do not open the envelope, scan the contents and put it aside to deal with later. Try to complete the task in one go.

If the content is an invoice, check it is correct, then put it on the Invoice Lever Arch File (this is explained in the chapter **Controlling The Finances**).

If the letter is a query of some sort that requires an answer, either: 1) phone (jotting down on the letter who you spoke to and what was said) or 2) write a note on the original letter, get a photocopy and post off the original letter with your note written on it or 3) type a letter in reply, keeping a copy. Use option 1) wherever possible for local addresses, option 2) for more distant addresses (comparing the cost of a telephone call to the cost of your time, a photocopy, envelope and stamp) and use option 3) where the matter is important and a proper written record is necessary.

Filing "Filing" is simply the grouping of similar letters and documents so you can find them easily at a later date. Grouping is normally done alphabetically A to Z in the same way as a Phone Book, so correspondence with a private customer, Mr Jim Scott, would be filed under "S" whereas correspondence with Mr John Smith, Administration Manager for Worthless Products Ltd would be filed under "W". Under "W" one would find any letters from Worthless Products Ltd and copies of letters from you to them. In addition to correspondence files you may have a few files for one-off or special subjects. For instance you may open a file, entitled "Raising Start-Up Finance" to enclose all correspondence, notes etc relating to that one topic.

TRING - A - LING
A·L·A·R·M·S

Tel: 01-123 456

**Number Ten
Sellers Lane
London EC1**

The Manager
Worthless Products Ltd
Unit 3
Industrial Estate
Birmingham B1 1ZZ

6 June 1990

Dear Sir

NEW RANGE OF SECURITY SERVICES

This letter is to introduce our company which has been set up recently.
We are offering businesses a comprehensive security service.

The two partners behind Tring-A-Ling Alarms have between them over 20
years experience in the security field and have both worked for well-
known companies in both technical and managerial capacities.

Tring-A-Ling Alarms can supply and fit locks, padlocks, window grilles
and other physical security devices. In addition we can install and
maintain electronic burglar alarms and closed-circuit television. The
latter can be of use to management as it permits you to observe the
loading bay doors during the working day.

I would like the opportunity to discuss your company's security
arrangements with you and I shall phone you in the near future.

Yours faithfully

A. Bell

A Bell
Sales Manager   **Partners: A. Bell, A. Clanger**

TRING - A - LING
A·L·A·R·M·S

Tel: 01-123 456

Mr A McSwindle
The Manager
Worthless Products Ltd
Unit 3
Industrial Estate
Birmingham B1 1ZZ

Number Ten
Sellers Lane
London EC1

14th June 1990

Dear Mr McSwindle

WINDOW GRILLES - QUOTATION

As a result of our meeting yesterday I have pleasure in providing you with the following quotation to supply and fit window grilles for your factory.

Quantity. Four windows - all to rear of premises facing railway line.

Specification. Mild steel expanded mesh as per sample left with you.
               Mesh to be attached to window surrounds by masonry nails.

Price. The total is £623.00 + VAT. This quotation is valid for 30 days.

Terms. Payment is due 7 days from date of invoice.

Guarantee. We guarantee our workmanship and materials for 12 months.

If you have any questions please do not hesitate to call me. I look forward to hearing from you in the near future.

Yours sincerely

A. Bell

A Bell
Sales Manager

Partners: A. Bell, A. Clanger

74

Doing Basic Officework

If you are unlikely to receive or generate much correspondence you could keep it all in a Lever Arch File (with stiff card A-Z separators) or an A-Z expanding pocket file. Otherwise you need to use conventional files.

Writing Business Letters

These should always be typed and you should keep a carbon copy (or photocopy) on file. A hand written letter looks totally unprofessional and would reflect badly on your business. If possible, letters should be written to a named person rather than a "Dear Sir" (which is less likely to get a response). Most letters consist of 4 parts:

1. Heading   This focuses the reader's mind. It should be in capitals and underlined.

2. Introduction   Normally one or two sentences describing the subject and referring, where applicable, to earlier correspondence or a meeting or phone call.

3. Main Body   This can be several sentences, several paragraphs (or in an extreme case, several pages!). It conveys the message of the letter. If it is a long letter or a quotation you can use sub-headings (or paragraph headings) as shown in the example opposite.

4. Actions   You have written the letter for a purpose. So in this final part of the letter there is a closing sentence or two stating what action(s) you want the reader to take and/or what action(s) you will be taking.

In a business letter one sometimes uses "we" unless you know the reader in which case it is more friendly to use "I". Finally, remember that if the letter is addressed as "Dear Sir" then it is signed "Yours faithfully" but if it is addressed as "Dear Mr Smith", it is signed "Yours sincerely". Refer to the two examples in this chapter which are first, from a new business trying to get work and second, a letter that is providing a quotation.

THE TELEPHONE

A great deal of business is done on the phone. Because phone bills can mount up alarmingly, try to make your calls, especially long distance calls, as short as possible (and ensure your staff do). If you are concerned about staff misuse of the phone, consider getting a small pay-phone These can be rented or purchased and suit some types of small business, especially where customers can use it too (eg in a hairdressing salon, café or guest house).

Phone Techniques

Often the first contact a customer has with your business is the person who answers your phone. The customer's impression is therefore coloured by how they are treated on the phone and you may gain (or lose) a sale as a result. It is essential therefore to use a good phone technique . . .

1. Answering   When answering do not simply say "Hello" or give your phone number. Instead, try "Good morning, (then give your business name), can I help you?" or maybe "Hello, John Smith speaking . . .", or maybe give your business name first, followed by your own name. Whatever you decide to say, take time to say it clearly and do speak as if you mean it!

2. Recording Messages   Many problems occur when phone messages are not written down. Orders can get mislaid . . . complaints are not dealt with . . . new sales enquiries do not get followed up, etc. Pre-printed telephone message pads are available from stationers. Make certain each phone has a pad and pencil nearby and ensure the *name* and *number* of the caller is always recorded.

3. Calling   If phoning a business: (a) avoid calling between about 1200 and 1430 hours as whoever you want may be at lunch. Friday after 1530 hours can be equally difficult; (b) ask for someone by name or ask for a department. Most larger businesses have similar department names – Sales, Purchasing, Finance (also called Accounts), Production, Design, etc and (c) remember to say who you are and equally importantly remember to get the name and possibly the job title of the person you are talking to so you can make contact easily again by name. It is quite important to build up a good personal relationship with your business contacts. (Selling by telephone is mentioned more fully at the end of the next chapter).

Mobile Phones   No longer just a "yuppie" toy, these can be very useful if you are often away from your office and need to keep in touch or you are expecting calls from customers. Choose your service provider carefully as there are some unscrupulous operators around and keep calls short as it is an expensive form of communication.

Telephone Answering Machines   If your office is left unattended for long periods and you are expecting calls, especially from potential customers, then a telephone answering machine would be a good investment■

Marketing and Sales

You do not have a business unless you can make *sales* and the whole process of getting those sales involves proper *marketing*. Analysis of the market and assessing the competition are also parts of marketing and were covered in the earlier chapter **Doing the Market Research**. Good marketing is vital to every business. When starting a new business the essential aspects are:

* Pricing your product or service.
* Advertising and promotion.
* Selling techniques.

PRICING

Too few businesses do this properly! First, the meanings of two important terms ... "Fixed costs" (also called "overheads"). This refers to business expenditure which is basically constant, ie "fixed" irrespective of the level of trading. So for instance, rent, rates, most salaries, insurance etc are all fixed costs. Overheads must be kept to a minimum as they can soon overwhelm the profitability of a business.

Overheads ... can soon overwhelm the profitability of a business.

"Variable costs" – (also called "direct costs"). This refers to expenditure which varies directly in relation to the level of business, for instance, costs of raw materials or stock.

PRICING PRODUCTS

A straightforward way to price a product is as follows:

1. If you are a manufacturer (This also applies to businesses such as catering where food products are made):

Selling price/unit =
(cost of raw material + direct labour + o/heads contribution) + mark-up + VAT

Cost of raw material: This should be relatively easy to calculate, but remember wastage. *Direct labour:* This is the realistic cost of employing staff to make the units, as shown in the following example. *Mark-up:* The mark-up (see also page 33) needs to be such that the manufactured items are sold at sufficient profit to cover the proprietors' or Directors' wages *plus* a small surplus (say 5-10%) to provide funds for future expansion, new product development or simply to save against any future contingencies. *VAT:* This is only added if you are VAT-registered and the product itself is VAT rated. *Overhead contribution:* This considers the overheads of the business, which obviously have to be supported by the production. It assumes everything that is made is subsequently sold (an important point).

Overheads contribution = $\frac{\text{total overheads}}{\text{total production}}$

Example: Assume you are self-employed making either small craft products, electronic devices, garments or whatever. Assume also the raw materials cost £10/unit and each item takes 1 hour to make, so in a 40 hour week you could make 40 such items. Now in this equation what should you allow for your labour cost? One answer is to charge what you would have to pay an employee to do the job. Why? Because if your business expands and you take on someone, had you been basing your selling price on a low labour figure you would then either have to suddenly raise your prices or reduce your profits – both undesirable. Now, if an employee's wage is £200 per week, then allow about 33% more to work out the hourly rate – why? Because you have employers National Insurance contributions, plus paid holidays, plus sickness and higher overheads. So in this example the direct labour cost would be (£200 + 33%)/40 = £6.65/unit.

Next, assume total overheads (ie rent, rates, insurance, phone, heat, light) come to £8,000 and total annual

production is 1,920 items (this assumes 48 weeks production, allowing you some holidays), then the overheads contribution/unit is £8,000/1920 = £4.17. Finally allow a mark-up of, say 10% (as you don't have any employees yet and the direct labour cost is in fact your "wage"), then the selling price is: (£10 + £6.65 + £4.17) + 10% = £22.90.

You might consider selling at £22.90 or a little more or less depending on the competition and the market.

In this example, the annual turnover (ie sales) = 1,920 x £22.90 = £43,968 which is below the current VAT threshold so the business would not need to be VAT registered and no VAT should be added to the cost.

KEY POINT Be cautious about pricing your product on the assumption that you will be operating at full production all the time for that is most unlikely.

2. If you are a wholesaler or retailer:

Selling price/unit = net cost price + mark-up + VAT (where applicable)

Example: If you buy an article for £4.65 net (ie without VAT added) and if the typical trade mark-up is 85% then the selling price = £4.65 + 85% + VAT which equals £10.11 (if the VAT rate is 17.5% and you are registered for VAT). There are four points to consider:

1. You may consider selling this article for £9.95 as that sounds more appealing to a customer.
2. Find out the typical trade mark-up percentages.
3. Keep your prices in line with your competitors.
4. Check the Cashflow Forecast reflects your mark-ups.

The effects of distribution on pricing How you distribute your product can make a great difference to your pricing, ie selling direct to a customer, using an agent on commission or distributing through a wholesaler or retailer can all make a difference. No way is best! Each is appropriate to a particular trade and you should know the mark-ups of the different distribution stages relevant to you so you can work out your "end-user" price to see if it is competitive. Some people when they start in business begrudge using wholesalers or retailers as they feel they will take too much profit. What they must realise is if they try to sell direct themselves it will take both time and promotion neither of which is cheap, and it might actually be better to sell indirectly through wholesalers or retailers who already have the outlets and the customers.

PRICING SERVICES

The pricing of services is normally based on hourly labour rates plus material costs. For consultancy or freelance work this is more usually called "fees plus expenses".

Calculating Hourly Labour Rates First of all find out typical "going rates" for what you are planning to do by asking people in the trade outside your area who are therefore not likely to be competitors. Next, if you plan to employ anyone, check that you can give them an adequate hourly wage out of that, making allowance for downtime and profit. Finally, insert that figure into your Cashflow Forecast by assuming you (and any employees) will be productive (ie doing work for which you can actually charge) for, say, 50% of the working week. The actual figure may be even lower and is unlikely to be much above 75%. By being productive for 50% means that in a typical 40 hour week you will only be charging for 20 hours but having to pay your staff for 40. The remaining 20 unproductive hours are absorbed in getting sales, doing paperwork, travelling, buying materials etc. If the Cashflow Forecast figure looks good and your labour rate is about that for the trade then that is a good start.

Materials Many people charge materials "at cost". You should be wary of charging for materials at what you paid for them because there are hidden costs you are ignoring such as the time you take to find and buy the materials, the cost of materials held in stock (ie the overdraft charges you may be paying for the stock), the cost of travel to pick up the materials, and so on. Some businesses define "at cost" being the retail price whereas they purchase the goods at wholesale prices thereby giving themselves some margin.

Estimates and Quotations An "estimate" is the approximate price of something, but usually a buyer will ask for a "quotation" and in writing. A quotation is a fixed price and if agreed is binding on both parties. See the sample letter in the previous chapter. As all quotations involve a degree of guesswork, you should carefully record your actual expenditure on the contract (by simply noting each day what man-hours and materials were spent on the contract). In this way your guesses should get better with experience.

General The vital subject of Pricing is explored in greater depth in a companion book, **"The (Greatest) Sales & Marketing Book"** – see the end of this book for details.

Marketing and Sales

Advertising Method	Cost	Good Points	Bad Points
Direct mailshot letter	Low	Targeted audience. High response rate (2% to 5% or perhaps more).	Time consuming to carry out, as it takes time to locate or produce a good mailing list.
Small Poster	Low	Large readership. Long life.	Limited to where posters are allowed. Message must be short.
Letterbox leaflet	Low	Can be part-targeted. Low response rate (usually well under 1%).	Difficult to distribute effectively unless done by eg Post Office, which increases the cost.
Directories (eg Yellow Pages)	Low/Med	Advert life is 1yr. Allows comparison with competitors.	Can only make changes annually and ensure you use a relevant Directory.
Direct mailshot leaflet	Low/Med	Targeted audience. Response rate is highly variable.	Time consuming to carry out (but less time than personalised direct mailshot letter).
Advert in local newspaper	Med	Local audience. Can repeat often. Usually some supporting editorial is possible.	Readership much larger than your target. Advert has to compete for reader's attention. Today's news, tomorrow's fish & chip paper!
Advert in trade publication	Med/High	Targeted. Editorial may be possible. Long life. Often a Reader Enquiry Service.	If publication relevant, none, except price.
Advert on Local Radio	Med/High	Wide audience. Suits certain consumer and business markets.	Advert life very brief so needs repeating frequently.
Advert in national newspaper or magazine	High	National audience. Can repeat often. Colour usually available on some pages.	As per local paper and editorial mention less probable. Ensure likely sales will cover costs.
Advert in "glossy" magazine	High	Some targeting possible. Full colour available on most pages.	Need to book space months ahead. High cost of advert production.

ADVERTISING AND PROMOTION

You can have a desirable product or service to sell at an attractive price but if nobody knows about it your business will obviously fail! There are many ways of finding customers and even a small business should use a combination of these. Some ways are more costly than others while some are more effective. Cost and effect are not always clearly related! The different methods are basically:

1. Advertising.
2. Issuing Leaflets & Brochures.
3. Producing Press Releases.
4. Taking a Stand at an Exhibition.
5. Doing Special Promotions.

ADVERTISING

First we can consider advertising. There are many ways of advertising (see Box above). With all advertising one is trying to target the message at the person who actually buys. Before advertising in a newspaper, magazine or Directory check to see if similar firms are advertising, if not it may be the wrong medium for you.

People tend to suppose that because they had a large half-page advert in the local newspaper backed up with some editorial, now everyone knows about their business – WRONG! It is a sad reality but people forget adverts almost as soon as they have read them. This is *unless* they happen to have a need at the *precise* moment they see the advert, so you would probably have to advertise regularly, ie weekly (or monthly if it is a monthly publication), but you

need not take large adverts, in fact a "little...often" is likely to give a better result than one or two big adverts.

Placing An Advert   For publications, phone the Advertising Department. Ask for their "advertising rates" which for the classified section will usually be quoted as cost/word or line and for display adverts are usually quoted as cost per single column centimetre (scc), which is a space one column wide and one centimetre deep. Display adverts are also quoted in terms of ⅛, ¼, ½ or full page. You should also ask by what date they need the advertisement. Ask them to send you a "rate card" which gives you all this information plus details of the circulation of the publication (ie how many people read it). If booking an advert, remember to send in a Press Release too (covered later in this chapter) as any editorial can be a great help.

Designing An Advert   Look at previous issues of the publication in which you plan to advertise and ask yourself − what catches the eye? It is very tempting to design an advert that seems to address itself to all readers − this is a "scattershot" approach and is rarely effective. Instead, address the advert to a specific section of the readership who will at least consider your product or service. Remember too the Trade Descriptions Act under which it is an offence to apply a false trade description to goods or services − in other words it must be honest and you must be able to prove any performance claims you make. Advertisments must never mislead.

If you are using a classified advert it needs a catchy heading. You can even take out two or more different adverts in the same issue − it is more effective than one long one. If you are placing a display advert remember a good photo or sketch is "worth a thousand words" so do use them. Remember too that as humans we respond most to photos showing people rather than inanimate objects.

Many new businesses give prominence in an advert to their company name but unless the name is very descriptive that is wasted for as a new business the name will have no impact, no meaning. However, if your company represents or sells a well-known brand name give that prominence (but do check first with the company concerned − they may even pay a portion of the advert). Another common error is to clutter the advert, yielding to the temptation to squeeze everything in. Remember the function of the advert is to arouse interest in specific readers and to encourage them

to take the next step (eg visit you). This latter point can be emphasised in the advert by putting a closing date or using words demanding action. But avoid saying "Act now!" in an evening paper unless you plan to man your phones or whatever that evening! An effective style of display advert is the pseudo-editorial advert that looks and reads like a news item. Despite the words PAID ADVERTISEMENT at the top, if written skilfully, it can be very worthwhile.

Designing adverts demands time, skill and experience. It is all too easy to get it wrong and produce an advert that yields too few sales. The subject is covered in much greater depth in **"The (Greatest) Sales & Marketing Book"**.

KEY POINT   Slick advertising cannot sell a poor product or change the fate of a poor business.

LEAFLETS & BROCHURES

The purpose of a leaflet (pamphlet or brochure) is to convey a message in a lasting form. An advert in a newspaper or magazine will last only as long as the publication sits around (since most readers are too lazy to cut out an advert). Leaflets can also carry a much longer message than an advert. The design breaks down into several headings ...

Size   This is a function of the amount of information you need to convey, the intended method of distribution (eg envelope size) and the amount you can afford to spend. It is best kept to a standard size, typically A4 (210 x 297mm), A5 (half A4 in size) or ⅓A4. It can be flat or folded and can be printed on one side or both sides.

Colour   A full colour leaflet is expensive. It is only justified if the product or service you are offering is itself expensive or needs colour to fully show its features (eg a wallpaper leaflet would be worthless in black and white), or if it needs to be in colour to compete with a rival's full colour leaflet. Note that you only use "full colour" printing if you are incorporating colour photographs and the printing cost is related to the number of such photos. If full colour is not essential great effect can be achieved by using a 2 or even 3 or 4 colour print. Remember that each colour requires a separate printing operation and so increases the price. Be careful of printing black on a gaudy coloured paper as these are often used to advertise cheap products or services.

The headline promises a nice benefit and may therefore catch the attention of more prospective customers than a specific heading eg "Garden Furniture".

Photos and illustrations are more convincing than words. Ensure scenes are lively and include people.

An introductory comment is required which clearly explains what is on offer.

The main part elaborates on the offer. Remember to add prices and give enough product information to arouse interest.

A call for action by an incentive is always useful.

If space permits you might advertise more of your range but never jeopardise the main offer by over-crowding.

Your business name would not normally be given emphasis unless it is particularly descriptive as to what you do.

Make the most of Summer with your Family and Friends

(space for colour photo, which extends under the heading above to create a large splash of colour. In this example the photo might show the furniture outside in the sun with a few happy people around and the heading above could be printed over the sky).

Garden Furniture — Huge Stock!

We can now offer a complete choice of attractive, comfortable and yet affordable garden furniture in pine, aluminium or plastic. Elegantly designed and carefully made to be enjoyed and admired. Chairs from £19.95, tables from £49.95.

Special Offer: 20% discount if you bring this leaflet and buy at least one table and 4 chairs before 31st May 1990.

We also stock a full range of pots, potting mixes, tools, seed, hoses, fertilisers, gravel, seedling trays, sprays, plants, greenhouses........

John Smith Garden Centre
Rose Street, Anytown
Tel: 01-234 567

For the Greenest of Gardens

(Fictitious Example)

This leaflet would probably require printing in colour to maximise its impact.

A little white space helps avoid the cramped, crowded look.

If your leaflet has a lot of text, it is important to arrange it in well spaced blocks so that it is easy to read. Prospective customers will not stop to read text which needs deciphering.

A map may be important when you are not located in a town centre site or are hard to find.

If you have a business slogan or motto you could add it.

Material   One can print on thin paper or thicker card with either matt, semi-matt or gloss finish. The thicker the paper the more expensive it is but it does have a better feel.

Information   A leaflet should read like a letter:

1. Heading. To focus the reader's mind. This is in large type and can either be descriptive, eg GARDEN FURNITURE or questioning, eg NEED SMART NEW GARDEN FURNITURE? or assertive, eg GARDEN FURNITURE NOW IN STOCK or indicating a benefit, eg MAKE THE MOST OF SUMMER WITH YOUR FAMILY AND FRIENDS.

2. Introduction. Normally a short paragraph explaining the heading.

3. Main Body. This could be several paragraphs or even several pages but do remember your reader may be a busy person so keep it as short as possible and try to make it interesting.

4. Call For Action. You are producing the leaflet because you want it to trigger some reaction. The end of the leaflet should therefore urge the reader to do something, such as contact you — by phone or letter, so your address and phone number should be given clearly. As we are all lazy and hate writing letters a simple reply coupon is useful.

Design   For any leaflet to achieve maximum effect the design must be good and it is suggested that professional help be sought when drafting it.

Folder   This is a specialised style of "leaflet", suitable where you are dealing with a small customer base, say under 100 or so, and the product or service you are supplying is complex or changing. The idea is to print a smart folder of lightweight card, usually A4 in size. Into this folder you can slip photocopied sheets of information, possibly an introductory letter and, where applicable, photographs. The folder gives impact to your presentation while maintaining maximum flexibility, by allowing you to add to or change the information sheets within it.

Distributing Leaflets This is very dependent upon your product or service and who are your likely customers. Here are some alternative ways of distributing leaflets:

a) Post through letter boxes (business addresses or homes).

b) Use the Post Office to deliver (they currently charge £45.50 per 1,000 leaflets and have a minimum charge).

c) Insert as loose in newspaper or magazine (they charge for this). Particularly popular with trade publications.

d) If your target market is local consumers, your local newsagent may, for a small charge, include them with the paper round.

e) Hand out in the street or at special events that attract your type of customer (but check if you need permission).

PRODUCING PRESS RELEASES

See the example over the page. It can be very worthwhile sending a Press Release to all relevant publications whenever you have something that is newsworthy. Include clear black and white photographs (they prefer 5x7 inch or 6x8 inch photographs) if possible featuring people because the human element is important to the media. If sending a photo remember to type a clear description of what the photo shows (especially the names of people) and stick the description to the back of the photo.

In Press Releases do *not* use superlatives or make suspect claims (eg "...the world's cheapest..."). Also, as shown in the example, quotes from relevant people are appreciated. Journalists prefer warning of events but if you do not want premature publicity you can use an embargo note on the top of the Press Release — this is a polite request to the publication not to print anything on the subject until the date shown on the embargo.

A good piece of editorial is worth a dozen adverts but do remember that: a) the publication may or may not use your news item, b) they may choose to use it days/weeks later, and you have no control over that, and c) they will write the article in their own words and with their own bias which may not be to your liking!

Trade publications are more likely to use your editorial than the consumer press but here are a number of hints to increase the chances of your Press Release being used: (a) Try to tie-in your news with some bigger event or story that the publication is already running; (b) Keep the Press Release short (under a page) and written to catch the eye and hold the reader's interest; (c) Put the most important aspect in the first paragraph (as any editing is usually done from the bottom up); (d) If available, a good photograph often helps and (e) Follow up the Press Release by phoning the appropriate Editorial department — not always a popular strategy but it can work.

PRESS RELEASE

SIMPLY PERFECT

12 Regent Crescent
Greenock
PA1 1ZZ
Tel: Greenock (0475) 242

LAUNCH OF NEW FASHION VENTURE IN GREENOCK

At a short ceremony in Greenock today, Miss Petunia Smart, well-known
actress, opened the new fashion boutique called SIMPLY PERFECT.

The shop, located at 12 Regent Crescent in Greenock, will stock ladies outerwear for
the mature successful woman. The range will include smart dresses, attractive skirts
with many co-ordinating blouses, dashing coats, head-turning hats and an extravaganza
of accessories.

Miss Joan Smith, 42, the proprietor of the new shop and a former teacher, said "At
present many ladies have to travel 18 miles to Paisley to look for smart outfits and
casual wear. I hope this new shop will meet their needs locally". Joan Smith has
visited the fashion houses in Paris, Milan and London to select her stock.

TV Personality, Miss Smart, who lives locally, said "I always need to dress well for
my TV appearances and I will certainly be making use of SIMPLY PERFECT. I spotted some
nice Italian blouses with floral prints".

The Director of the local Enterprise Agency, Mr Helpful, said "We are delighted to have
been able to assist Miss Smith with this venture. We helped her to prepare the necessary
Business Plan and provided other general start-up advice. This is our 100th new business
start-up that we have helped".

To introduce local ladies to the new stock, there will be a fashion show at a
Hotel on the 10th May. Tickets are available from the shop.

FOR FURTHER INFORMATION:

Miss Joan Smith
Tel: Greenock (0475) 242

PHOTOGRAPH attached

Proprietor: Joan Smith

Shop Hours: Mon-Sat 0930-1730

Fictitious example

Marketing and Sales

EXHIBITIONS & OTHER PROMOTIONS

Exhibitions.. Participating in Exhibitions, Consumer Shows and Trade Shows has become of increasing importance. For non-retail businesses they provide regional, national or even international exposure. However, many new exhibitors are disappointed with the results of their initial showings. This is mainly due to inexperience and unrealistically high expectations. (It might also be, one should add, that their product or service is not viable).

Exhibiting requires a great deal of preparation, an adequate budget and hard work before, during and afterwards to make the most of it. The decision to participate should not be made on the spur of the moment.

Essential preparation includes: a) visiting a number of similar exhibitions and talking to the organisers; b) deciding which show(s) to exhibit at; c) designing stands; d) organising leaflets and exhibits; e) deciding on any supporting publicity to encourage people to visit you; f) working out manning rosters and booking accommodation; g) reading the fine print of the exhibition rules and h) training staff how to sell effectively from the Stand.

Seminars/Talks/Demonstrations These can be very useful if you get the *right* audience. It can be used for many different businesses including both manufacturing and service industries. You need to think carefully who your likely buyers might be then invite them to an occasion where you can have their attention and give them your sales "pitch".

If you are selling to trade buyers then you may be able to tag on to some other event (eg a trade association or Chamber of Commerce meeting). If not, to get the buyers to come you need to make the occasion sound interesting and appealing — perhaps lunch or drinks at a nice hotel may encourage them to come.

If you are going to this effort to set up such an important occasion you should ensure that your presentation is good, ie a good speaker, good visual aids (maybe a video or slides), samples on display and leaflets for people to take away. If possible try to have a full rehearsal beforehand.

Monitoring Your Advertising & Promotion Whatever method of advertising or promotion you use, as it is costing you time and money you should monitor the results. For leaflets or newspaper adverts one can say something like "Bring this leaflet (or advert) to get 10% off" or with leaflets an idea is to make a secret mark on several of the leaflets distributed with a note on the leaflet that whoever brings in a leaflet so marked will get a (desirable) gift.

Where the buyer has to write, as in mail order, an old trick is to use a fictional department in the address so you know that replies addressed to "Dept M" were in response to a certain advert. If you are actually meeting customers (eg in a retail situation), ask politely how they heard about you.

With all monitoring write down and analyse the results. Here is a fictitious example for a shop:

68 customers were asked how they knew about the new shop of whom 12 people (18%) saw an advert in the local newspaper, 15 people (22%) heard about the shop by word-of-mouth, 26 people (38%) were just passing the door and came in and 15 (22%) were already repeat customers.

SELLING TECHNIQUES

There is a saying that customers "buy benefits, not goods or services". What that means is best illustrated by an example. A soccer fan may buy a video recorder because he wants the benefit of being able to replay his favourite matches. If there was some other way he could do that he might not be buying a video recorder. In other words it is not really the video recorder he needs and is buying, but the benefit it gives him. It is worth bearing the concept in mind when you are trying to sell something.

This section covers successful selling techniques which, if applied, will help you overcome any fears you might have and will assist you achieving that essential ingredient of all businesses — more sales!

Remember too (and remind staff) that it is your customers who provide your income and your staff's wages — so make customers feel important — they are!

1. FACE-TO-FACE SELLING (NON-RETAIL)

This could be "cold calling", ie you do not have an appointment or it could be a pre-arranged meeting. In any event, before you set out: (a) dress smartly; (b) gather adequate sales material and know it thoroughly; (c) have price lists to hand and (d) leave on time so as not to be late.

Sales material is a key element of face-to-face selling. It consists of samples, brochures, your business cards, order forms and possibly a calculator if you need to come up with estimates or quotations on the spot. If you do not have a

Marketing and Sales

good brochure and it is not possible to carry samples due to their size, an effective substitute is a photo album with clear pockets into which you slip a piece of blank paper onto which are fixed photos with a typed description. The photo album can also contain newspaper cuttings, letters of commendation (testimonials), certificates of technical competence and so on. Of course you need not show every page to every customer.

Handling The Meeting Here are some tips for the actual sales meeting:

* There is no need to be nervous as people enjoy chatting and you have an excellent product (or service) to sell.

* Don't run up stairs or along corridors as it will make you out of breath.

* Don't have a drink beforehand to steady your nerves as the smell can be noticed and gives a poor impression.

* On meeting the "prospect" give a firm handshake and hand over your business card if you've not met before.

* In a business context, if you are not sure of the "prospect's" name or job, ask for his or her business card.

* Listen to find out the customer's *needs*. If you can match those needs, explain how your product or service can achieve that.

* If the customer raises objections, this is healthy and the objections should be listened to carefully. It may help you to jot down what is said so you can overcome objections one at a time without missing any.

* Close the sale, get the buyer to sign a copy of the order form and leave them a duplicate copy of the order which should include the agreed price and timescales.

Note: The Consumer Protection (Cancellation of Contracts Concluded away from Business Premises) Regulations 1987 provide for a 7-day cooling off period in which agreements covered by these Regulations can be cancelled by the consumer. Get a leaflet from your Trading Standards Officer.

Techniques For Closing The Sale You must learn to be able to sense when a customer is ready to buy — he or she may start to ask detailed questions or talk about methods of payment. Then you can attempt to close the sale by, for instance:

1. Take out your order book (very visibly) and ask something like "so, how many **** do you want in your first order?" or "on what date would you like your first order delivered?" (and then discuss quantities).

2. Another technique is to bypass the yes/no decision completely by discussing details of the order, getting the customer involved and then take out your order book.

If the customer says he needs to "sleep on the matter" before he decides, then leave something like your personal catalogue (marked ONLY COPY) or samples which you arrange to collect the next day (or the day after, ie don't let it cool too far!). This tactic allows you to see the customer face-to-face again which gives you a second opportunity to close the sale and it is much more difficult for the customer to turn you down in person, than over a phone.

If the customer is unsure because he needs a boss's or colleague's opinion, ask for that colleague/boss to join your discussions or arrange to come back and see them all (ie try not to let them decide in your absence!).

If the customer says he needs to sleep on the matter
... leave your samples ...?

84

2. FACE-TO-FACE SELLING (RETAIL)

Small retail outlets fall into two categories — "convenience shops" (such as a newsagent, corner shop or chemist) and "specialist shops" (such as a boutique, gift shop or TV and electrical shop). In a convenience shop the customer tends to make most of his or her purchasing decision *before* they enter and in a specialist shop the customer tends to make his or her decision *after* they enter. That is a crude simplification but it emphasises the differences in selling. In the former case there is little "selling" as one is primarily responding to the customer's requests, though selling can still play a part by encouraging the customer to buy additional (often complementary) purchases.

Let us concentrate though on the specialist shops where selling plays a greater role. Here are some suggestions:

1. Always acknowledge the presence of a customer very soon after they enter the shop, by a nod, smile and possibly a "Hello" or "Good Morning" even if you are already dealing with another customer. This makes them feel more at home on unfamiliar territory (especially if they have not visited the shop before) and it also tends to "hold" them until you are free to help them. It is a simple strategy and yet ignored by many shops.

2. Let the customer browse for a few moments and then approach them. Do not say "Can I help you?" as you will get the universal reply "No, I'm just looking!" which stops your sales pitch dead in its tracks. Instead, try using a question more related to the situation. For instance, if a lady is looking at blouses, you might ask "Is the blouse to match a particular skirt?...what colour?...day wear or evening wear?...". In a gift shop, you might ask "Is it something for yourself or a birthday present?...". The point of these questions is they tend to open up a dialogue which has several advantages: a) it stops the customer rushing around the shop and disappearing out the door, b) it allows you to find out what the customer *needs*, c) it allows you to offer your goods to match those needs and d) the customer will think you are being helpful. On the other hand, being too pushy can of course lose sales.

3. The show window is a crucial factor in selling from a specialist shop. The window is the magnet that draws people in (very often on an impulse) so it should be bright (actually lit up with lots of lights), attractive and articles on display should be clearly priced. The window should be changed weekly or fortnightly and it should have a theme such as a subject or a common colour. For ideas, look at the windows of the big department stores (who all have full-time professional window dressers) and take notes to use for your own shop.

4. Sales material you should have includes showcards and posters or stickers which are produced by the suppliers of the stock you are carrying. They may also provide leaflets.

5. Layout. The shop layout is important to assist your selling and should be discussed with shopfitters who know about retailing your type of goods. In particular, thought should be given to point-of-sale displays as these can contribute significantly to your turnover.

3. TELEPHONE SELLING

The telephone is a most useful tool to back up your sales drive, however to use it effectively requires skill and practice. There are courses available for tele-sales techniques which could be worth attending. The main advantages of selling by phone are: a) you can contact a large number of people in a relatively short time and b) you can often get through to the decision maker. Its main disadvantages are: a) you cannot show your product or other sales material to the customer and b) you cannot see their facial reactions.

As with any sales work, preparation is essential, so you must know who you are calling and what you are trying to achieve with the call. The phone conversation should be handled in very much the same way as any sales meeting so in your opening statement you would identify yourself and your company. You should also state clearly what is the purpose of your call. This opening statement should be rehearsed but not recited parrot-fashion. So should your fact-finding questions and sales message. Several other hints are as follows:

1. Try to keep a smile on your face.
2. Keep your product/sales information in front of you.
3. Remember the customer will be thinking "What's in this for me?"
4. Understanding the customer's business is half the battle.
5. Close the sale, or where appropriate, arrange an appointment to see the customer.
6. Since there is nothing in writing, always summarise what has been agreed and later confirm in writing if necessary.
7. Bear rebuffs bravely — don't get rude or angry.
8. Pause then put the phone down after the other person.
9. Keep a record of all your calls■

Exporting

Why Export? Businesses start to export for different reasons – good reasons include the desire to make the most of a good product or service which is applicable to a wider market than just the UK. Another reason is as a precaution in case there is a downturn in the UK economy. A less good reason might be to try selling something abroad because it is not selling well enough in the UK.

Some companies actively pursue an export policy and produce a Business Plan with that venture in mind, while other companies slip into exporting because they have been approached by an overseas buyer and this slowly leads to other export sales.

Government, naturally enough, tries to encourage exports, but the proprietor of a small business cannot afford to be dazzled by the sales pitch. Also, though there is much promotion of the European Single Market, there are of course many important markets outwith Europe, notably North America. As a small business it may be wise to focus initially on one small export area rather than trying to take on the whole world!

Who Should Think of Exporting?

First of all, a small company should probably not consider exporting unless either the company is well established in its home market making it financially strong enough to set out on this new adventure or one of the proprietors has been in this field before and "knows the ropes". This therefore does not exclude new or recently started businesses.

Exporting can be exciting, though the initial glamour of jetting around the world and staying in hotels etc can wear thin. It certainly can provide enormous opportunities even for the smallest of businesses – provided they have the right things to sell.

Exporting, however, is not something to simply dabble in!

GETTING INTO EXPORT

Market Research As with any new business venture, the first thing to do is to find out more about the market, ie to do some market research. There are people who can help (speak to your Enterprise Agency or business development unit), but one good and quick way is to visit an appropriate trade show in the country concerned. Speak to people in the trade over there and get copies of relevant foreign trade publications (from which you can have selected articles translated later).

It may be that your product will require modifying to suit specific overseas markets. Find out too if you will require an import licence for the country concerned, if there are any import duties and if you require an export licence from the UK (such licences are needed only for a limited range of items).

Distribution Assuming your market research results are encouraging, for

---

Some Advantages of Exporting

Market Size Obviously one of the biggest advantages is the potential market is larger than simply this country.

Market Match The product or service you are selling might suit certain overseas markets better than the UK.

Eggs in several baskets Selling in markets beyond the UK provides a possible "hedge" against a downturn in this economy.

Currency Advantage Although outwith your control, a change in currency exchange rates can give you a definite selling advantage if Sterling is weak against your customer's currency.

Some Disadvantages of Exporting

High Costs It's very expensive travelling abroad to get orders. Expensive in management time too. It's also expensive shipping goods and paying Agent's fees which raises your prices and may make them uncompetitive.

Market Mismatch Culture, customs and language can all be different to what you are used to – sometimes quite alien. This has the practical problem that a successful product or service in the UK might be of little use or interest to people abroad.

Regulations Obviously you need to know what local regulations apply. There may also be import restrictions or onerous duties.

Shipping Procedures There is a lot to learn!

Currency Disadvantage It was mentioned above that a fluctuation in exchange rates can be beneficial, equally it might not be!

Unpaid Debts A potential problem facing businesses which export is collecting debts. This can be a very serious problem.

Exporting

manufacturers you need to consider the options to market your product:

1. Agent. An agent will visit potential customers, take orders (usually on a 10% commission) and then you ship the goods direct to the customer and invoice these customers direct. Finding a good, reliable agent and controlling customer debt are the main problems.

2. Distributor. A distributor not only goes out taking orders but also stocks your goods. You then only have to ship goods to (and invoice) the distributor. As with agents, they should not only sell your goods but also provide important feedback from customers.

One way to find an agent or distributor is by recommendation through your trade association. Alternatively the Department of Trade and Industry operate the "Export Representative Service" which for a fee will provide a list of possible representatives.

3. Sell Direct. This can be done by taking a Stand at a Trade Show abroad and hopefully taking orders direct from customers. Again, just as with the first option above, you would have to ship and invoice each customer individually. Follow up sales might be difficult or just too expensive for you to undertake, but if you attend the Trade Shows regularly, customers can come to expect to see you there.

4. Collaborative Projects. A completely different approach is some form of collaboration with an overseas company. This might take the form of you providing certain facilities or contacts for them in exchange for them providing the same for you.

5. Manufacture Under Licence. In this case an overseas manufacturer agrees

Here's the supply boat .... I wonder what today's exchange rate is for coconuts?

to make and sell your product locally. You could supply parts to them or even the whole product in kit form. Alternatively you may just get paid a royalty. This is complex legally and needs good advice. It is essential to fully check-out the other party's track record, financial status and integrity.

Services: The above options are mainly for manufacturers. For a service business, the options depend very much on the type of business concerned.

Trade Shows Even the smallest business can consider participating in international Trade Shows. First it is useful to go as a visitor to assess the Show and the competition. For selected overseas Trade Shows there may be some grant assistance available from the DTI for new exporters.

There are, of course, international Trade Shows held in the UK which

attract foreign buyers and a business can make a tentative move into exporting by exhibiting at one of these.

If looking for an agent or distributor abroad, you might display a small sign "Agent Wanted" in your Stand.

If you plan to make your contacts through an annual overseas Trade Show, a good rule-of-thumb is the first year you will not make enough sales to cover your costs, the second year you may, with luck, break even and in the third year you may achieve profit.

Pricing A major problem with exports is the extra costs that inevitably make your products more expensive abroad than they would be if selling at home. Even if you are selling on an "ex-factory" or "fob" basis, the end price of the goods will still be higher.

These additional costs include freight charges (and the often onerous handling and shipping agent fees); shipping insurance (always more expensive than when simply moving the goods within the UK); export credit insurance; import duties where applicable; and bank charges. There might also be an overseas agent's commission to add.

Hence a product which retails in the UK for £10 (with a 100% mark-up for the retailer) might be the equivalent of £12, £15 or more, on the shelves in another country. This can obviously diminish the appeal of your product unless the foreign economy can withstand the higher price or if the currency conversion is in your favour.

How To Send Goods For most products there are probably three options. The first option (if the goods are lightweight) is by post. This can be by air (which is relatively expensive but quick) or surface (which is cheaper but takes

87

Exporting

many weeks to most places). One big advantage is that you have no handling agent's fees, so for small orders this can be quite useful.

However, most exporters will have to consider using the two other options – air freight or sea freight. A good Shipping Agent is essential to handle the often complicated documentation and to advise on the best route and carrier – the most direct way is not always the best. If you are quoted a shipping cost in terms of £/kg (quite often its $/kg), then remember to ask about the handling charges which can add quite a lot to the overall bill.

ARRANGING PAYMENT

It is one thing to succeed in getting an export order, it is quite another matter to actually get paid for it! Certain countries seem to be notorious non-payers while others have the reputation of being excellent payers. Expert advice is required and this is available from the DTI's Export Credits Guarantee Department, 2 Exchange Tower, Harbour Exchange Sq., London E14 9GS, tel: 071-512 7000.

Whereas with a UK customer you might insist on payment by proforma (ie they pay before you send the goods)

the normal method for an unknown export customer is to use either a Letter of Credit or other documentary collection, which are handled through your bank and are relatively safe.

If you plan to offer credit, do remember to take up references just as you do with any UK customer.

Note that a bank will charge not only to arrange the transfer of cash (by eg Letter of Credit) but will also charge to convert a foreign currency payment into Sterling. To avoid the latter you could ask your customer if they can pay by "Sterling cheque drawn on a UK bank" – and if they are unable to do this then ask your bank what their conversion charges are likely to be.

AND FINALLY

If you are seriously considering exporting, as a first step you could speak to an expert provided through the "Enterprise Initiative" (see page 50).

In terms of "Business In Europe", there is further literature available from government, tel: 0272 444 888.

Note: If you are VAT registered and you want to trade with other EC states, you will discover to your dismay that there is additional VAT accounting and returns to be completed■

KEEPING GOING!

Chapters

Controlling the Finances

Business, by definition, is all about money and the proper management of that money is paramount to the success of any business. This chapter covers the operation of a business bank account, keeping records, how to keep a simple set of accounts and how to do Cashflow Management (based on the Cashflow Forecast you did for your Business Plan).

I said PROPHETS Isaiah, not PROFITS!

LEMONADE 20p

Business...is all about money

THE BUSINESS BANK ACCOUNT

The first principle to grasp is that it is vital to separate "business" money from "personal" money. It is rather like when a friend asks you to buy something for them and gives you a £5 note. You put this money in a separate pocket and after buying the item you return the change to that pocket keeping it apart from your own money — it is a simple discipline which prevents any embarrassing confusion. In a business context this separation is achieved by opening a business bank account and keeping any loose cash from the business in its own container which can be either a cash till or tin box clearly marked "Business".

Opening An Account Visit your Bank Manager and discuss opening the business account. He will want to know about the intended business, so you should be prepared — take him a copy of the Business Plan you have completed. In addition to wanting to know all about your proposed venture he will probably also want answers to the following questions:

Account Title This is the name which is normally printed on your cheques. If it is a limited company, then it is normally the company title in full. For a sole trader or partnership it can be the personal name(s) with, it is suggested, the words "BUSINESS A/C" added, eg "JOHN SMITH BUSINESS A/C" When a business name is to be used you could just have the trading name, eg "TRING-A-LING ALARMS" but it is better to have the proprietor's name(s) added like this: "A. BELL & A. CLANGER T/A TRING-A-LING ALARMS" (T/A means "Trading As"). The advantage of including your name(s) is that you may be able to use your personal cheque guarantee card with your business cheques, which would not be possible if only the business name is printed. But first ask your bank manager's permission to use the card in this context.

Signatures The bank will also ask who can be an authorised signatory to the bank account. If it is a partnership or there are two directors (in the case of a limited company) then the bank will want to know if one signature or two will be necessary on cheques and other authorisations. In this case it may be wiser to have two signatures required for each cheque or perhaps the bank could be instructed not to pass any cheque over, say, £100, unless there are two signatures.

Statements The bank will want to know how often statements are required, monthly is the most common (and is recommended), and to which address they should be sent.

Bank Finance The manager will want to know if you will be looking to the bank for finance. If this is the case then you should leave a copy of your Business Plan at the bank several days before your appointment to give the manager time to read it.

Opening Deposit Finally, to get the new account open, the bank will normally request a deposit of money from your personal funds.

Writing Cheques Cheques are often written out very carelessly with the high risk of either the cheque being tampered with or the bank innocently debiting a wrong amount. It is also vital to keep track of the value of the cheques you have written. If your cheque book has stubs, one good tip is to write on the next unused cheque stub the total amount left in the account after writing each cheque. This means you are always aware of how much is left and you are never in danger of overdrawing the account.

Always "cross" your cheque with two bold diagonal lines and the words *A/c Payee Only* written between the lines. Your cheques may come pre-printed as such. Also if you

Controlling the Finances

have to give someone a blank cheque then write clearly somewhere on the cheque "Amount not to exceed £25" (or whatever value is relevant).

One last point on the subject of cheque writing and it may seem like stating the obvious, but it is absolutely crazy to write a cheque when there are no funds in the bank account (it is also an offence!). The repercussions of this folly can be horrific – the bank will "bounce" the cheque and your lines of credit will dry up as suppliers get nervous. Worse still, your bank will think that you cannot control your finances and they may withdraw any overdraft facility you might have with potentially terminal results for your business.

Handling Money Many new businesses that handle actual cash create difficulties for themselves when cash received from customers is used partly for business purposes and partly for purely personal items, with no proper records being kept. A good habit is to pay all the money you receive (ie cash

and cheques) into the business bank account. When you want to "pay" yourself you write a cheque to yourself "John Smith", and if you need to buy something for the business you would normally pay by cheque. However, if you are only buying something costing say, less than £5, then two alternatives are:

1. Petty Cash Writing cheques for small amounts is not only time consuming but potentially expensive in bank charges. If you think you may need to buy a total of £50 of small purchases then you cash a cheque for £50. Put the money into your "petty cash box", buy the items you need, get receipts for everything and keep a note in the appropriate columns of your Accounts Book.

2. No Petty Cash An alternative is to use your personal money for the various purchases, keeping receipts for everything as before. Then at the end of every week or month you total up

the receipts and write yourself one cheque, made out to "Cash", to reimburse your private pocket for the purchases.

Unless your business involves a great deal of purchasing of small items the second method is preferable as it involves less paperwork and effort.

Bank Statements Each month the bank should send you a statement. Statements should be filed neatly together and kept in a safe place as your accountant will want to see them when doing your annual Tax Return.

The statements should always be checked to see: a) the correct amounts have been credited and debited; b) what bank charges and other D/Ds (Direct Debits) have been deducted and c) that any direct credits have indeed been paid into your account.

The Direct Debits and any Direct Credits should be written up without delay in the Accounts Book and the running total on your cheque book stub should be updated too.

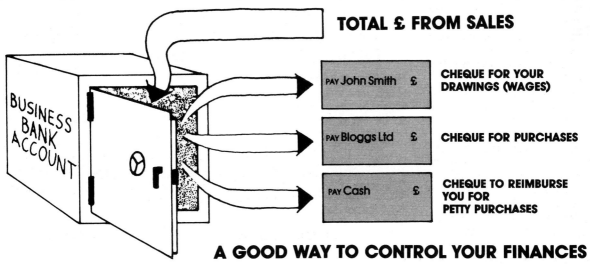

TOTAL £ FROM SALES

PAY John Smith £ — **CHEQUE FOR YOUR DRAWINGS (WAGES)**

PAY Bloggs Ltd £ — **CHEQUE FOR PURCHASES**

PAY Cash £ — **CHEQUE TO REIMBURSE YOU FOR PETTY PURCHASES**

A GOOD WAY TO CONTROL YOUR FINANCES

KEEPING RECORDS

Keeping Receipts (Invoices) You need to keep the receipts for *everything* you buy in connection with your business. Despite using the word "receipt", an "invoice" is usually acceptable and more common when payment is made by cheque. Here for simplicity we shall just use the word "invoice" to mean both.

Invoices should be filed in some manner. One suggestion is to keep the invoices paid by Petty Cash in an envelope (one for each month) and to use a 2-hole lever arch file for the invoices paid by cheque, as shown right. Cheque invoices should be filed in *cheque number* sequence. Write the cheque number boldly on an outside corner of the invoice so that it can be cross-referred to easily.

You can use a card divider in the lever arch file to separate *paid* from *unpaid* invoices. File unpaid invoices on one side of the card, and when you pay them, move them to the other side of the card. This should prevent you from forgetting to pay any bills.

Rather than simply using an envelope for your Petty Cash invoices you could use another 2-hole lever arch file, but in this case the invoices would be filed in *date order* and simply numbered in sequence starting from 001.

The purpose of keeping receipts (ie invoices) is so that you have proof of purchase and can justify those expenses to the taxman. Note that a proper invoice should give the supplier's name and address, date, amount and a proper description of the goods or service supplied. It should also have an identifying number. Other than for small amounts, it should also give the purchaser's business name.

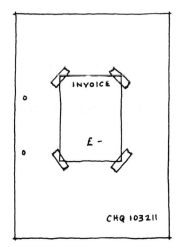

A receipt (invoice) which is too small to fit the Lever Arch file can be mounted first on a piece of blank A4 paper.

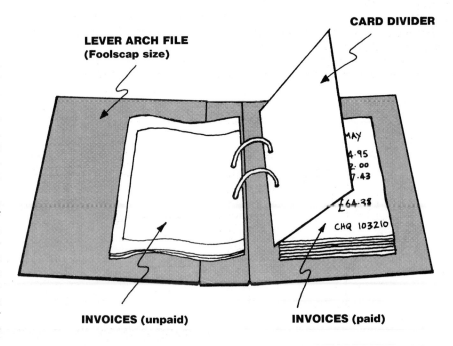

CARD DIVIDER

LEVER ARCH FILE (Foolscap size)

INVOICES (unpaid)

INVOICES (paid)

Controlling the Finances

If VAT-registered, the invoice must also carry the issuer's VAT number and the VAT rate. For invoices over £100 the total (less VAT) and the VAT charged should be shown separately.

KEY POINT Keep receipts (invoices) from the earliest stages, even before you actually start trading.

Keeping A Record Of Purchases If your business grows and you find you are buying a lot of goods or services on credit then you may find it difficult to keep track of what is happening. A solution is to start a book called a "Purchase Ledger". The format of this varies from business to business but a suggested layout is shown opposite. You could either simply buy a lined hardcover book and draw your own columns or you could buy loose-leaf pre-printed ledger pages, but in either event only record what you have to and modify your recording system if it is not to your liking.

Keeping A Record Of Sales In every business you should have a record of your sales as proof for the taxman or VAT man, and for your own information. In a retail context this record could be the cash till roll, while in other businesses it could be the duplicate copy of all the invoices you issue. Invoices should be numbered in sequence. You can purchase carbon duplicate invoice books from any stationers. Simply write your name and address (and VAT number if registered) on the top of each page or use a rubber stamp or printed label to save time.

If you are offering credit, ie not being paid immediately, you should have a good record of who owes you, how much, and how long the bill has remained unpaid. This record is called a "Sales Ledger" and a suggested layout is shown opposite. As with the Purchase Ledger it could simply be a hardcover book with your own columns drawn on it. See also the notes on the Consumer Credit Act in the chapter **Making It Legal**.

Keeping Other Records Your accountant (and maybe a tax or VAT inspector) will normally also want to see your business bank statements, pay-in books, cheque book stubs and a list of goods taken from the business for personal use. Ask your accountant in advance what records he or she will want to see at the end of your tax year. (Note: If you employ any staff, you will need to keep further records relating to PAYE. Refer to the next chapter).

KEEPING SIMPLE ACCOUNTS

Who Does What? As many people know little about keeping accounts when they start in business, they hope their accountant will "do the books" for them. This is not necessarily ideal for two reasons. First, and most importantly, knowing your exact financial situation is essential to managing any business and if you, your spouse, or one of your staff keeps your books then you ought to know how matters are fairing. Second, using an accountant to do your books will be expensive.

When you *should* use an accountant is: a) for advice before and in the early stages of setting up the business, b) to

---

USEFUL GLOSSARY

Credit Note   Often looks like an invoice (and hence confusing) but it is in fact an I.O.U. and is issued if, for example, there is an over-payment by the customer or a customer returns defective goods.

Delivery Note   A contents slip included with goods that are delivered or collected (usually on credit).

Invoice   The bill issued to you when you buy something so you know how much you have to pay. Or the bill you issue to your customers.

Receipt   A slip confirming that the invoice has been paid. Not always issued these days when payment is made by cheque, credit card or by post, but a receipt is useful when payment is made by cash.

Remittance Advice   This is a slip (often attached to a Statement) which is then returned with a cheque so the recipient knows who the cheque is from and what it's for.

Statement   Normally issued monthly to a customer who is buying on credit. It summarises the invoices issued and payments received.

PURCHASE & SALES LEDGERS

Notes:

1. Use one page per supplier/customer.
2. File suppliers pages together — these form the PURCHASE LEDGER.
3. File customers pages together — these form the SALES LEDGER.
4. A ledger is like a bank account statement, so in a Purchase Ledger when you buy £75 of goods this is shown in the "Credit" column and when you pay your suppliers the payment is shown in the "Debit" column.
5. In contrast, with a Sales Ledger, when you sell £50 of goods this is shown in the "Debit" column and when it is paid for by the customer their payment is shown in the "Credit" column.
6. (*) In the column below marked "Ordered By" you could use a single letter to indicate how the order was placed, eg T — placed by telephone, L — placed by letter and V — a verbal instruction.

PURCHASE LEDGER

Suppliers Name: .... Your Account No: ....

Address: .... Credit Limit: £ ....

Tel. No: .... Any Special Factors: ....

Contact: Mr/Mrs/Miss .... Job Title: ....

Date	Your Order No.	Ordered By (*)	Description	Goods Received	Invoice Received	Debit	Credit	Balance	Notes

SALES LEDGER

Customers Name: .... Account No: ....

Address: .... Credit Limit: £ ....

Tel. No: .... Any Special Factors: ....

Contact: Mr/Mrs/Miss .... Job Title: ....

Date	Customer Order No.	Ordered By (*)	Description	Goods Sent	Invoice Sent	Debit	Credit	Balance	Notes

Controlling the Finances

help create your book-keeping system, c) for taxation advice once the business is started, d) to do your annual accounts and Tax Return and e) if necessary, to help you raise money for expansion.

BOOK-KEEPING SYSTEMS

Keep It Simple! There are many different ways of keeping accounts and any way is acceptable provided you, your accountant, the tax man and (if registered for VAT) the VAT man, can understand it! It is essential that you yourself understand the system as some small businesses have failed partly because their book-keeping system was so complex that the proprietor could not understand it.

Single Book or Multi-Ledger? When you start in business you will probably only need to keep a single Accounts Book, but as your business grows you may need to consider moving to more complex (and expensive) systems. Usually the move to a multi-ledger system occurs not because your turnover has reached any particular level but because you need more "control" of purchases and sales made on credit, which in practice usually means the control of slow-paying customers.

Not surprisingly, operating a multi-ledger system takes much more time as it involves double-entry book-keeping, and its users often ultimately consider computerising their accounts – see the chapter **Using a Computer**.

Multi-ledger accounts systems are outwith the scope of this book as they are usually of less relevance to a new-start small business.

Single Accounts Book Systems

Every business needs an Accounts Book to record the funds received and payments being made. It is sometimes

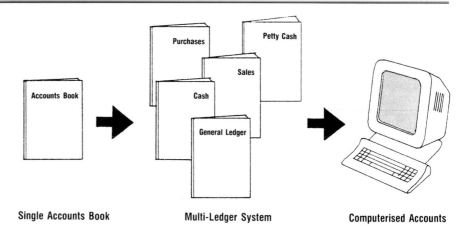

Single Accounts Book   Multi-Ledger System   Computerised Accounts

FROM A SIMPLE ONE-BOOK "SYSTEM" TO EVER-MORE COMPLEX SYSTEMS AS A BUSINESS GROWS

referred to as a Cash Book and it should relate to the bank statements, sales receipts and purchase invoices.

There are a number of single Accounts Books designed for the smaller business. The books fall into two categories: (i) those which are pre-printed so the user only has to fill in the figures where directed (like the example opposite) or (ii) "blank" accounts books which are merely ruled with lines and columns but have no headings or instructions and therefore require some knowledge of book-keeping.

ACCOUNTS BOOKS

First we look at some pre-printed Accounts Books on the market:

1. The Best Small Business Accounts Books (Price about £7.99 and available from most branches of W.H. Smith or mail-order direct from Hingston Associates. See the last page in this book for ordering details).
These two Accounts Books are from the publishers of "The Greatest Little Business Book". They are intended to be the simplest and easiest to follow

on the market and have been designed specifically for non-VAT registered small businesses (see page 98 for a VAT version).

Different types of business need different designs of accounts books and hence there are two in this series.

They have colour coded covers – the YELLOW BOOK is for a *cash business with daily sales* and is ideal for small shops, many self-employed, driving instructors, market traders etc. A page from the YELLOW BOOK is shown opposite (reduced in size) and there is one such page for each week of the year.

The BLUE BOOK is for a *credit business where sales are mainly invoiced*. It is ideal for small manufacturers, consultants, freelancers, agents, tradesmen, importers, builders etc. Pages from the BLUE BOOK are shown on pages 100-102 (reduced in size). There are four pages to each month.

Other businesses such as guest houses, office service businesses, craft-workers, caterers, vehicle repairers etc. can choose whichever book best suits their style of operation.

The Best Small Business Accounts Books

In this series, there are two accounts books for non-VAT registered businesses and one accounts book for a VAT business. The illustration (right) is from the YELLOW BOOK which is for a non-VAT *cash* business with daily sales. Each week has one full page.

The BLUE BOOK (shown on pages 100-102) is for a non-VAT *credit* business where the sales are mostly invoiced.

Normally A4 (210 x 297mm) in size the page has been reduced to fit here.

Week 1

commencing . . . .

MONEY RECORD

	£	p
Money in hand at start of week		

DAILY TAKINGS		
Monday		
Tuesday		
Wednesday		
Thursday		
Friday		
Saturday		
Sunday		
Total Takings		

OTHER MONEY, LOANS etc		
Cash from Bank		
Total		

WEEK'S MONEY BALANCE		
Money at start of week plus Daily Takings plus Other Money, Loans etc		
Less Total Bankings		
Less Cash Payments		
Leaves: Balance		

Money in hand at end of week		

Discrepancy ±		

© 1991 P. Hingston

BANK RECORD

	£	p
Bank Balance at start of week		

DAILY BANKINGS		
Monday		
Tuesday		
Wednesday		
Thursday		
Friday		
Saturday		
Sunday		
Total Bankings		

BANK DIRECT DEBITS etc		
Cashed Cheques		
Charges/Interest		
HP/Lease/Loan		
Total		

WEEK'S BANK BALANCE		
Bank Balance at start of week plus Daily Bankings less Bank Direct Debits plus Bank Credits		
Less Chq Payments		
Leaves: Balance		

BANK STATEMENT CHECK		
Balance (from above)		
Not yet on Statement: Add total cheques Less total bankings		
Leaves:		

PAYMENTS RECORD

	PAID BY CASH			PAID BY CHEQUE		
	Ref	£	p	Ref	£	p
Stock/Raw Materials						
Stock/Raw Materials Sub-Total						
Advertising/Promotion						
Business Insurances						
Cleaning						
Drawings/Salaries/NI/Pension						
Electric/Gas/Heat						
Fees (eg Accountant, Lawyer)						
Motor – Fuel						
– Repairs/Service						
– Tax/Insurance						
Postage/Parcels						
Rates						
Rent						
Repairs/Maintenance						
Staff Wages						
Staff PAYE/NI						
Stationery/Printing						
Sundries						
Telephone/Fax						
Travelling						
Other Expenses						
CAPITAL EXPENDITURE						
Total Cash & Cheque Payments						

Controlling the Finances

In both the YELLOW BOOK and the BLUE BOOK there are full instructions, worked examples and a special feature of the books is their "self-balancing" columns. These make it much easier to calculate the money and bank balances.

At the end of each book are simple summary sheets to complete at the end of the tax year. An accountant would need these in order to complete the Tax Return. *The Best Small Business Accounts Books* are suitable for Sole Traders, Partnerships or Limited Companies.

2. The Best VAT Business Accounts Book *(Price about £8.50 + VAT, available from most branches of W.H. Smith or mail-order direct from Hingston Associates. See page 120 for order details).*

To complement the Best Small Business Accounts Books, there is a self-contained VAT version of the BLUE BOOK. With a similar format but with additional columns for VAT and a new section to list VAT Inputs and Outputs. There are also sections to record trade with other EC Members. The VAT Account has been specially designed to make the completion of VAT Returns much easier.

3. The Simplex D *(Available from most stationers, price about £6.75).* This book is primarily for small non-VAT registered businesses which have transactions, ie purchases or sales, almost daily. The book provides one page per week and contains instructions and example specimen pages. There are also end-of-year summary sheets at the rear.

If using a Simplex D and your business grows and you need to register for VAT then you can use their special "Simplex VAT Record Book" in conjunction with the Simplex D.

4. Collins Complete Traders Account Book *(Available from most stationers, price about £16).* This is designed for VAT-registered shops. It contains instructions and example specimen pages. The book also has sections to permit you to calculate and record your VAT. Collins also produce the similar *Self-employed Account Book* for businesses not concerned with cash retailing.

5. Twinlock Complete Accounts Book *(Available from most stationers, price about £16).* This is an accounts book suitable for many VAT-registered businesses. It is a loose-leaf binder style of book which has the advantage that you can add sheets. It has instructions and worked examples.

Blank Heading, Ruled Accounts Books. Pre-printed Accounts Books as mentioned so far can be used by virtually anyone without book-keeping experience (with a little coaching from their accountant or business counsellor). In contrast, the blank heading, ruled type of accounts book requires someone with suitable book-keeping knowledge to set up and may be more difficult for the novice to comprehend. However, once mastered, they are more flexible.

Available from most stationers are the *Cathedral, Guildhall* and *Cambridge Analysis* books, priced from about £10 to nearly £20 (depending on size).

These books are suitable for both VAT or non-VAT registered businesses and come in different sizes (A4, A3.5 and A3), in different thicknesses (ie with more pages) and most importantly, with differing numbers of columns. Each page is identical. Choose a book with enough columns to suit your business – your accountant can advise you.

AT YEAR END

In addition to the routine book-keeping you have been doing throughout the year, at the "year end" there are important, but relatively simple, additional tasks to carry out. (The "year end" refers to the end of your financial (tax) year, rather than the calendar year).

For instance, if you hold any stock, raw material or part-completed work, you need to do a stock-take on the last day of your financial year. A "stock-take" involves counting all the different items you have and valuing them (normally at cost price). Another task is to list all your business creditors (ie people you owe money to) and debtors (ie people who owe you) as of that date.

Some of the better pre-printed accounts books have suitable pages and instructions to help you with these end of year tasks.

COMMON BOOK-KEEPING PROBLEMS

Here are several typical problems you might encounter when doing your own book-keeping: (1) If you are a sole trader or partner and use your private car or home telephone partly for business use and wish to recover the business element of this expenditure, then you could pay these bills by business cheque, keeping a record of the business usage and at the end of your tax year you should be able to claim that proportion of the expenses. (2) If you pay for any business items using your personal credit card, when the card statement arrives, simply pay for the business items using a business cheque. (3) If you are unsure if an invoice is regarded as a "business" expense, either ask your accountant or note it on the appropriate page of your accounts book. (4) If you trade as a sole-trader or partnership and want to transfer some surplus money into a deposit account, then enter it in the Accounts Book under "Drawings" (it should not affect your tax liability). (5) If you are using one of the blank heading, ruled accounts books, you may wonder what column headings to use. This question is best answered by your accountant.

Two other points. If a figure in your

accounts is negative (eg a bank balance in overdraft) this is normally shown by brackets, eg (£100) means -£100. Secondly, if you are *not* VAT-registered, then throughout the Accounts Book you should record the full invoice value, inclusive of any VAT charged.

And Finally . . . .

Do try very hard to keep your book-keeping up-to-date. If you find you are slipping behind, don't give up – stop what you are doing and try to fill in something very easy such as the current week's figures. Once you have broken the ice, go on to catch up with the past weeks you have missed.

CASHFLOW MANAGEMENT

The Objective One of the most common reasons a small business gets into financial trouble is due to "cashflow problems". This usually occurs when goods (or services) are bought on credit and later when the bills come in there is no money (or overdraft facility) to meet those bills. Cashflow problems may also result from the business having too little work or suffering from bad payers.

In every business, cash comes in..... but so do the bills and it can soon become difficult to control. This is where Cashflow Management is useful as it helps you to forecast your future cash requirements and any problems can be spotted early and something done about it.

Cashflow Management is in fact a very simple technique and once mastered you will really wonder how anyone can run a business without it.

Finally, never confuse cash *inflow* with *profitability*. Money sitting in your shop's cash till or your bank account may be needed to cover bills. However, a profitable business can still have cashflow problems if its customers are slow in paying. And remember that the bottom line of a Cashflow Forecast does not represent either a "profit" or a "loss".

How Does It Work? You will have prepared a Cashflow Forecast for your business before you start (or you ought to have!). Have a look at the Cashflow Forecast prepared for the fictitious shop "Simply Perfect" which you will find in the chapter **Preparing the Business Plan**.

If this was your business, then at the end of the first month shown on the cashflow (May in this example) you would add up the actual amount under the different headings in your Accounts Book (which should match the headings being used in your cashflow) and insert those into the cashflow. See right.

Very quickly you can spot that the May sales were much lower than forecast (£605 actual instead of £1000 forecast). So you would revise downwards your June forecast to perhaps £1000. The net effect is that the likely overdraft by the end of June is going to reach £2,483 unless urgent action is taken – and action is necessary since the overdraft limit is only £2,000.

If this was your own shop, the action you would have to take might include cutting back on stock purchases and talking to the bank about temporarily increasing your overdraft limit. But the key question is why are the sales lower than anticipated and what can be done about that?

In this way each month you would update your cashflow, inserting the actual figures for the month just passed and changing figures ahead where known. The continuing changes make the arithmetic tedious and the whole operation is made more acceptable by using a simple spreadsheet program on a small computer as discussed in the later chapter **Using a Computer**■

Cashflow for fictitious shop "Simply Perfect"

	CASH IN	MAY	JUN
1	Sales (inc VAT)	605	1000
2	Bank or other Loans		2000
3	Owner's Capital	6500	
4	Other Money In		
5	TOTAL	7105	3000
	CASH OUT (inc VAT)		
6	Stock/Raw Materials	5122	3000
7	Advertising & Promotion	187	
8	Bank Charges/Interest		
9	Business Insurance	350	
10	Drawings/Salaries/NI		300
11	Electric/Gas/Heat		75
12	Fees (eg Accountant, Lawyer)	300	
13	HP/Lease/Loan Payments		80
14	Motor – Fuel		
15	– Other Expenses		
16	Postage/Carriage		
17	Rent & Rates	1000	250
18	Repairs & Maintenance		50
19	Staff Wages		
20	Staff PAYE/NI		
21	Stationery/Printing	31	
22	Sundries	96	50
23	Telephone/Fax	248	50
24	Travelling		
25	VAT		
26	Other Expenses		
27	CAPITAL EXPENDITURE	1263	136
28	TOTAL	8597	3991
29	Net Cashflow	(1492)	(991)
30	Opening Balance	0	(1492)
31	CLOSING BALANCE	(1492)	(2483)

© 1991 P. Hingston

The Best Small Business Accounts Books

In this series, there are two accounts books for non-VAT registered businesses and one accounts book for a VAT business. The illustrations (right and next two pages) are from the BLUE BOOK which is for a non-VAT *credit* business where the sales are mostly invoiced.

Each month has 4 pages and these are illustrated (in reduced size) on this and the following two pages.

NOTE: The BLUE BOOK is now available in a VAT VERSION (not shown here). The layout of the BLUE VAT BOOK is the same as the non-VAT version except there are additional columns to allow for VAT, an extra 32 page VAT section and help to complete your VAT Returns.

The YELLOW BOOK (shown on page 97) is for a non-VAT *cash* business with daily sales.

Normally A4 (210 x 297mm) in size the page has been reduced to fit here.

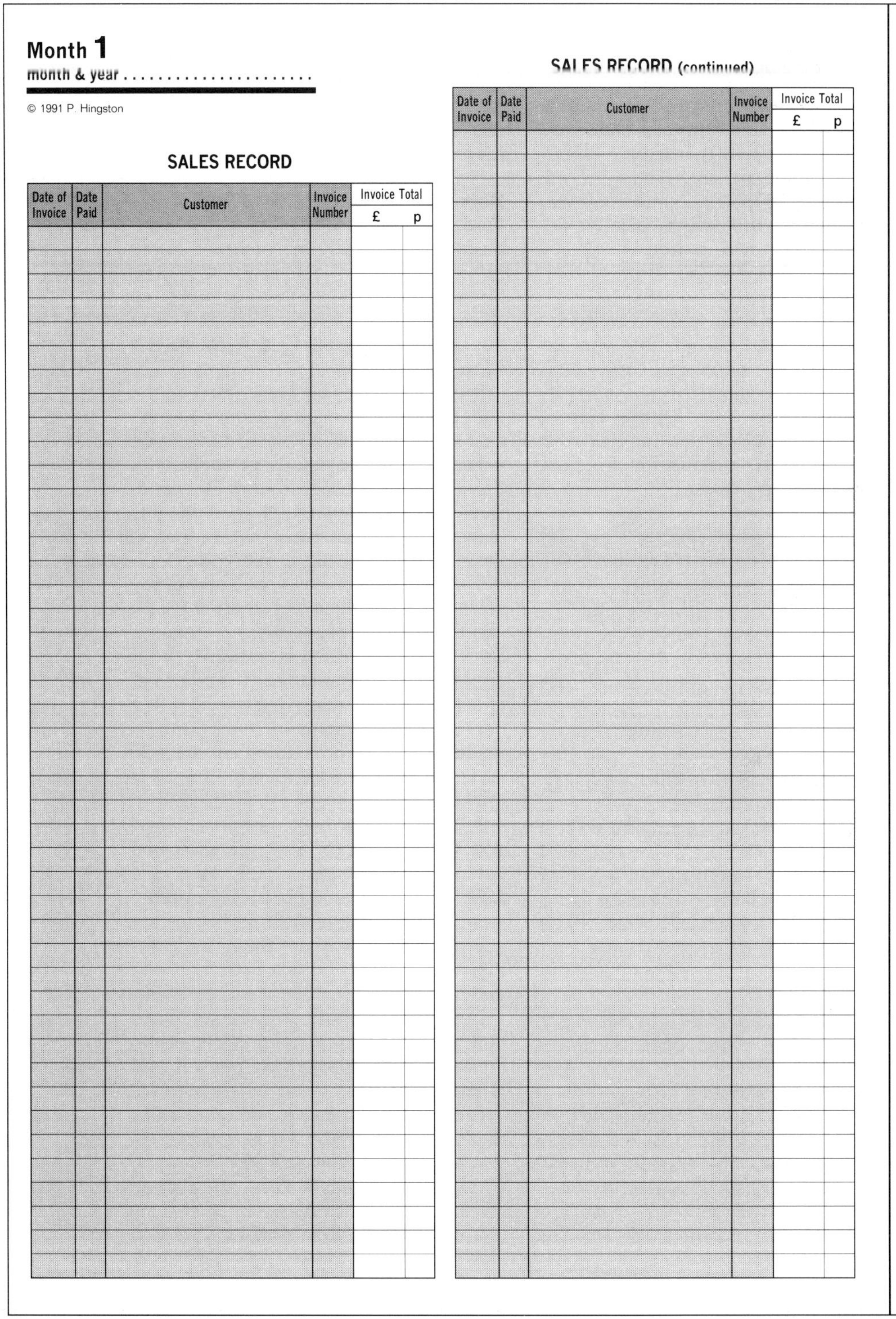

Month 1
month & year ....

© 1991 P. Hingston

SALES RECORD

Date of Invoice	Date Paid	Customer	Invoice Number	Invoice Total £	p

SALES RECORD (continued)

Date of Invoice	Date Paid	Customer	Invoice Number	Invoice Total £	p

BANK RECORD

PETTY CASH   © 1991 P. Hingston

	£	p
Bank Balance at start of Month		

BANKINGS			Non-Sales		Sales	
Date	Details	Ref	£	p	£	p
	Direct Credits					
Totals						
Total Bankings (ie Total Non-Sales + Sales Bankings)						

BANK DIRECT DEBITS etc			
Date	Details	Ref	
	Bank Charges/Interest		
	HP/Lease/Loan repayments		
Total			

MONTH'S BANK BALANCE & STATEMENT CHECK		
Balance at start of Month + Total Bankings − Direct Debits		
Less Total Cheque Payments (total from overpage)		
Leaves: Balance at end of Month		
BANK STATEMENT CHECK	Add total cheques not yet on Statement	
	Less total bankings not yet on Statement	
	Leaves: Balance as per Statement	

	£	p
Money in Petty Cash at start of Month		

MONEY INTRODUCED DURING MONTH		
Date	Source of Money	Ref
Total		

PAYMENTS BY PETTY CASH		
Stock/Raw Materials		
Advertising/Promotion		
Cleaning		
Drawings/Salaries		
Electric/Gas/Heat		
Motor − Fuel		
− Other Expenses		
Postage/Parcels		
Rent/Rates		
Repairs/Maintenance		
Staff Wages		
Stationery/Printing		
Sundries		
Telephone/Fax		
Travelling		
Any Other Expenses		
Total Payments by Petty Cash		

MONTH'S PETTY CASH BALANCE		
Petty Cash at start of Month + Money Introduced		
Less Total Payments by Petty Cash		
Less any surplus Cash paid into Bank		
Leaves: Money in Petty Cash at end of Month		

Each month in the BLUE BOOK is given four pages. Below is illustrated page 3 and part of page 4 (shown here very much reduced in size).

Month 1 .... **PAYMENTS BY CHEQUE** (Note: There are overflow pages after Month 12) © 1991 P. Hingston

Date	Cheque Paid To	Chq No	TOTAL		Stock/ Raw Material	Advertising/ Promotion	Drawings/Sal/ NI/Pension	Electric/ Gas/Heat	All Motor Expenses	Postage/ Parcels		Rent/ Rates	Staff Wages & PAYE/NI	Stationery/ Printing
Total Cheque Payments for Month														

Coping with Taxation

This chapter shows you how to cope with Income Tax and National Insurance contributions (including PAYE), Corporation Tax and VAT. Please note that this is not a comprehensive guide to these taxes, aspects of which are highly complex and details of which change. Regard this chapter therefore as an introduction to the subject to help you cope with routine aspects of these taxes. To check details speak to your accountant or the relevant government department who you will normally find most helpful. Note too that these are not the only taxes that might confront you – for instance there is Capital Gains Tax which could apply should you make a gain on selling a business asset such as property. For your convenience we have produced at the end of this book a **Tax Data Page** which gives details of the current rates of taxes and other data. Refer to it as you read this chapter.

WHO PAYS WHICH TAXES?

Everyone in business is subject to taxes, but depending upon the legal form of the business and whether or not there are employees, dictates which taxes are relevant and how these taxes are collected. So who pays what? ...

Sole Trader or Partnership (no employees) In this case Income Tax is based on the business profits as declared in the annual Accounts, and the Income Tax becomes due for payment in two instalments (January and July).

In the case of a partnership, the profits of the business are divided equally between the partners unless the Partnership Agreement says something to the contrary, but the liability for paying the tax is met by the business.

In addition to Income Tax, a sole trader or partner is liable to pay Class 2 National Insurance contributions which are a fixed weekly amount and Class 4 contributions which are profit related and calculated as a percentage of the profits in your Tax Return. (Class 4 contributions are therefore collected the same time as Income Tax). The Class 2 contributions are best paid by direct debit through your bank.

Sole Trader or Partnership (with employees) In addition to the above, if you have full-time employees (defined as a person who earns more than a certain weekly amount) then you must deduct National Insurance (and pay an Employers contribution) for these employees. If they earn more than a second (higher) amount then PAYE (Pay-As-You-Earn) also has to be operated so that any Income

Tax due can be deducted. The operation of PAYE is covered later in this chapter.

Limited Company As a salaried Director of a company, you will almost always have to operate the PAYE system for yourself as well as any full-time staff you employ. The Income Tax and the National Insurance contributions are paid through the PAYE system – see below. In addition to these taxes a limited company is also liable to Corporation Tax which is a tax on profits, paid usually 9 months after the accounting period.

HOW THE TAXES ARE COLLECTED

We now consider each of the main taxes in turn...

INCOME TAX (For Sole Traders or Partnerships)
Consider the following example. Assume your total annual sales (ie "turnover") is £50,000 but you had to spend £40,000 on stock purchases, staff wages, rent/rates and other overheads, then you would have made a profit of £10,000. That would be declared in your Tax Return and the £10,000 is then regarded as the equivalent of a wage of £10,000. You are still entitled to your normal "personal allowances" and what is left is taxed at the prevailing rate of Income Tax.

...What is left is taxed at the prevailing rate of Income Tax.

Coping with Taxation

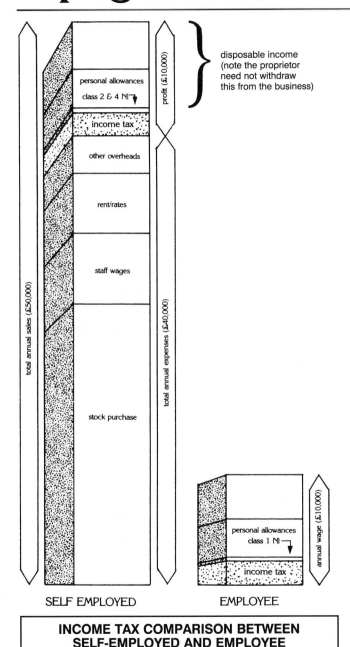

disposable income
(note the proprietor
need not withdraw
this from the business)

personal allowances

class 2 & 4 NI

income tax

other overheads

rent/rates

staff wages

stock purchase

total annual sales (£50,000)

total annual expenses (£40,000)

profit (£10,000)

personal allowances

class 1 NI

income tax

annual wage (£10,000)

SELF EMPLOYED

EMPLOYEE

**INCOME TAX COMPARISON BETWEEN
SELF-EMPLOYED AND EMPLOYEE**

Note that it makes no difference how much money you actually draw from the business − £25 per week or £250 per week, as your liability to Income Tax is solely dependent upon the *profitability* of your business!

The example we have discussed is shown graphically on the left.

Allowances In the above example we deducted £40,000 in costs from the £50,000 annual sales figure to arrive at the profit figure of £10,000 on which income tax is due. But what types of expenditure and "overheads" can you deduct? For income tax purposes an important distinction is made between "revenue expenditure" and "capital expenditure". Broadly speaking, "revenue expenditure" covers consumables and wages which would all normally be allowable deductions. This includes purchasing of stock or raw materials, staff wages, rent, rates, phone bills, electricity and heating charges, advertising, stationery, insurance, professional fees, the replacement of worn-out tools by similar tools, interest on business loans and most vehicle expenses.

"Capital expenditure" covers once-off purchases of tangible assets such as buildings (including alterations), equipment, tools and vehicles. These are *not* automatically allowable − only certain categories are allowable, which are given a general writing-down capital allowance of 25%. The rules for buildings are more complex. Note that with cars you cannot claim back the VAT you pay when buying one even if you are registered for VAT. In contrast, with vans you *can* normally reclaim the VAT.

Only revenue expenditure which is wholly and exclusively for your business can be deducted from your annual sales figure when calculating your taxable profits. However there are frequently situations where expenditure is partly for business and partly for domestic purposes. Examples include the use of a car, the use of a telephone at your home and heat and lighting used in an "office" in your home. In the case of a car (or van) you could keep a vehicle running log book in which you record every business trip (ie Date, Destination, Mileage and Purpose of Journey). In the case of a telephone you could also keep a log of all business calls you make (ie Date, To whom, Local/District/Trunk, Time of Day and Call Duration). In this way you will have the necessary proof to claim the correct proportion of the charges against tax. However, before you start to log anything, do speak to your accountant as you may be

giving yourself an unnecessary burden.

Items which are *not* allowable for Income Tax purposes include: your own drawings (ie your "wages"), household food or other domestic expenditure, Income Tax, National Insurance contributions, business entertainment etc.

Construction Industry 714 Tax Certificate
If you plan to work self-employed as a sub-contractor in the construction industry you may need to apply for this certificate. Without such a certificate the main contractor has to deduct tax at the basic rate from all payments and this may make obtaining sub-contract work difficult. Contact your local Inland Revenue office for more details.

Coping With Income Tax
Provided you keep the accounts recommended in the chapter **Controlling the Finances**, and you use an accountant to advise you, then you should be able to cope. The Inland Revenue's pamphlet IR28 is very readable and provides good advice for sole traders and partnerships. Remember to keep money aside to pay your tax! If your turnover is low, the Inland Revenue will accept simplified "three line accounts" (see page 117).

NATIONAL INSURANCE (Sole Traders/Partnerships)
Even if you have employees you have to pay your own Class 2 contributions separately (employees pay Class 1 contributions – see **PAYE** below). Visit your nearest Social Security office and ask for the appropriate leaflets for a self-employed person. You can elect to pay your Class 2 contributions monthly by direct debit from your bank account.

The Class 4 contribution which is based on the profitability of your business is generally assessed and collected by the Inland Revenue at the same time as your Income Tax. The Class 4 contribution is calculated as a percentage of the profits exceeding a certain figure but there is a maximum contribution limit.

PAYE (Ltd Companies & all full-time Employees)
PAYE stands for Pay-As-You-Earn and is Income Tax and NI (National Insurance) deducted by an employer from the employee's wage packet. You will also have to pay an employer's NI contribution. If you employ staff or are a limited company contact your nearest PAYE office (look under "Inland Revenue" in the Phone Book), and ask them for a "New Employers Starter Pack" which contains full

instructions and forms. To see how this works in practice, look at the worked example later in this chapter.

Paying PAYE/NI   When you register for PAYE you will usually be sent a Payslip Booklet with which you can either pay the amount due at your bank or post a cheque. The amount should cover both the Income Tax and National Insurance, including the employers contribution. Most employers have to pay this monthly but if your monthly payments are below a certain threshold you can elect to pay quarterly. For further advice, contact your PAYE office.

CORPORATION TAX
This is only relevant to limited companies and is a tax on the profits of a business in much the same way as Income Tax is calculated for a sole trader or partnership. Corporation Tax is normally paid nine months after the end of the accounting year.

If as a Director you take a wage out of the company, the wage will be liable to Income Tax which will have to be deducted from your wage packet under the PAYE scheme mentioned above. Shareholders in the company can be paid "dividends" out of the profits of the company but the tax rules are complex with ACT (Advance Corporation Tax) having to be paid by the company – this requires your accountant's advice.

VALUE ADDED TAX (VAT)
First refer to the item on VAT in the **Making it Legal** chapter. The VAT "bible" is the VAT Guide (Notice 700) which will tell you all you need to know about VAT and a lot more besides. Remember that you do not need to register for VAT unless your taxable turnover exceeds (or is likely to exceed) a certain figure. See the **Tax Data Page** on page 117. Registration is also required if at any time it appears you will exceed the threshold in the next 30 days. How VAT works in practice is shown in the Box over the page.

If you need to register for VAT then you must keep additional records to those you would otherwise keep for the business. In particular you need to record all taxable goods and services that you buy and sell as part of the business. There is no set way to do this but they must be such that you can fill in your VAT Return each quarter and so the VAT man can understand them. Ask your accountant about this or ask the local VAT office. In addition as a VAT-registered trader you will have to give proper tax

Coping with Taxation

> A VAT-registered trader buys goods for £100 to which VAT at 17½% is added so his bill is £117.50. The £17.50 is called his "input" tax which he can reclaim later. When he sells the goods he puts a mark-up on them and sells them for, let us say, £200. Since he is VAT- registered the £200 will include VAT (the actual amount is found by multiplying £200 by 7/47 which is called the "VAT fraction" and it equals £29.79). The £29.79 is called his "output" tax. When completing his quarterly VAT Return, on that one transaction he would owe £29.79 in VAT but he can reclaim £17.50, so the net amount he has to pay the VAT man is: £29.79 – £17.50 = £12.29.
>
> Note: One way to remember the VAT fraction of 7/47 is to think of a Boeing 747 Jumbo jet.

The "Cash Accounting Scheme" This special scheme allows a small business to account for VAT on the basis of payments received and made rather than tax invoices issued and received. This can be a particular help if you give your customers long periods of credit.

The "Annual Accounting Scheme" Small businesses with a taxable turnover less than a certain threshold may be eligible to opt for this scheme whereby the business can account for its VAT by making nine monthly payments by direct debit, and sending in one annual VAT Return with a tenth payment, adjusted to balance the account.

For more details on both these schemes, contact HM Customs & Excise■

invoices unless you sell direct to the public in which case you only need to provide a tax invoice if requested. The VAT leaflet "Keeping Records and Accounts" gives more information and is very readable.

Note that as a VAT-registered trader you can normally only reclaim "input" tax if you have a proper tax invoice.

If you are registered for VAT then you must normally make a return to the Customs & Excise each quarter on a Form VAT 100 (usually referred to as the "VAT Return"). Refer to the specimen form opposite. You have 30 days from the end of the quarterly period to complete the form and return it together with a cheque (if you owe VAT). If your input tax exceeds your output tax total, then once you have submitted your VAT Return you can expect a cheque from HM Customs & Excise. Finally, do remember that there are stiff penalties for late submission of VAT Returns.

Tax Point An important aspect to remember when completing the VAT Return is the "Tax Point" (ie date) of a transaction. In practice this is normally the date given on the invoice (provided the invoice is raised promptly) but note that legally this is only one of the possible relevant dates, ie when goods were supplied or a service completed are other possible Tax Points. Provided a Tax Point is within the quarter on which you are reporting then it has to be included in your VAT Return (even if no payment has yet been made!) unless you are using the "Cash Accounting Scheme".

HM Customs and Excise

Value Added Tax Return
For the period
to

For Official Use

SPECIMEN

Registration number

Period

You could be liable to a financial penalty if your completed return and all the VAT payable are not received by the due date.

Due date:

For official use D O R only	

Before you fill in this form please read the notes on the back and the VAT leaflet *"Filling in your VAT return"*. Fill in all boxes clearly in ink, and write 'none' where necessary. Don't put a dash or leave any box blank. If there are no pence write **"00"** in the pence column. **Do not** enter more than one amount in any box.

For official use

			£	p
VAT due in this period on **sales** and other outputs	1			
VAT due in this period on **acquisitions** from other **EC Member States**	2			
Total VAT due **(the sum of boxes 1 and 2)**	3			
VAT reclaimed in this period on **purchases** and other inputs (including acquisitions from the EC)	4			
Net VAT to be paid to Customs or reclaimed by you **(Difference between boxes 3 and 4)**	5			
Total value of **sales** and all other outputs excluding any VAT. **Include your box 8 figure**	6			00
Total value of **purchases** and all other inputs excluding any VAT. **Include your box 9 figure**	7			00
Total value of all **supplies** of goods and related services, excluding any VAT, to other **EC Member States**	8			00
Total value of all **acquisitions** of goods and related services, excluding any VAT, from other **EC Member States**	9			00

Retail schemes. If you have used any of the schemes in the period covered by this return, enter the relevant letter(s) in this box.

If you are enclosing a payment please tick this box.

DECLARATION: You, or someone on your behalf, must sign below.

I, ...declare that the
(Full name of signatory in BLOCK LETTERS)

information given above is true and complete.

Signature ....Date ....19...............

A false declaration can result in prosecution.

CD 2850/N3(04/92)   F3790 (JANUARY 1993)

VAT 100

Crown copyright. Shown here reduced in size. Reproduced with the permission of the Controller of HMSO.

107

PAYE WORKED EXAMPLE (Fictitious Employer & Employee)

| Deductions Working Sheet P11 | Year to 5 April 19 **94** | | Employee's surname in CAPITALS **SMITH** | First two forenames **JOHN** |

Employer's name WORTHLESS PRODUCTS

Tax District and reference

Complete only for occupational pension schemes newly contracted-out since 1 January 1986.
Scheme contracted-out number

| S | 4 | | | | | | |

National Insurance no **AA 12 34 56 A**

Date of birth in figures — Day Month Year
Works no. etc
Date of leaving in figures — Day Month Year

Tax code † **344L**   Amended code†
Wk/Mth in which applied

National Insurance contributions*

PAYE Income Tax

For employer's use	Earnings on which employee's contributions payable 1a	Total of employee's and employer's contributions payable 1b	Employee's contributions payable 1c	Earnings on which employee's contributions at contracted-out rate payable included in column 1c 1d	Employee's contributions at contracted-out rate payable included in column 1c 1e	Statutory Sick Pay in the week or month 1f	Statutory Sick Pay recovered. Only complete this column if you are claiming Small Employer's Relief 1g	Statutory Maternity Pay in the week or month included in column 2 1h	Month no	Week no	Pay in the week or month including Statutory Sick Pay/Statutory Maternity Pay 2	Total pay to date 3	Total free pay to date (Table A) 4a	Total 'additional pay' to date (Table A) 4b	Total taxable pay to date i.e. column 3 minus column 4a or column 3 plus column 4b 5	Total tax due to date as shown by Taxable Pay Tables 6	Tax due at end of current period. Mark refunds 'R' 6a	Regulatory limit i.e. 50% of column 2 entry 6b	Tax deducted or refunded in the week or month. Mark refunds 'R' 7	Tax not deducted owing to the Regulatory limit 8	NET WAGE For employer's use
									6 April to 5 May	1											
										2											
										3											
										4											
									6 May to 5 June	5											
	130	16 43	7 82							6	900 00					113 96					
										7	130 00	1030 00	464 31		565 69	124 42			10 46		111 72
										8											
									6 June to 5 July	9											
										10											
										11											
										12											
										13											
									6 July to 5 Aug	14											
										15											
										16											
										17											
									6 Aug to 5 Sept	18											
										19											
										20											
										21											
									6 Sept to 5 Oct	22											
										23											
										24											
										25											
									6 Oct to 5 Nov	26											
										27											
										28											
										29											
										30											
	Total of w'd	Total of w'd	Total of w'd	Total of w'd	Total of w'd	Total of w'd	Total of w'd														

SPECIMEN

P11(1993)

* You must enter the NI contribution table letter overleaf beside the NI totals box - *see the note shown there*.

† If amended cross out previous code.

∅ If any week/month the amount in column 4a is more than the amount in column 3, leave column 5 blank.

Assume you've taken on a new employee, John Smith, and on his first pay day (Friday 21st May) his gross wage is £130. First prepare a Deductions Working Sheet (as shown above) using the information supplied on Smith's Form P45, such as the £900.00 and £113.96. (Note: If your new employee has no P45, refer to the instructions given in the PAYE P8 Guide). To calculate his net pay:

Col 1a Insert Smith's weekly earnings in this column.

Now open the National Insurance Not contracted-out contributions Tables CF391 (see top Table extract opposite).

Cols 1b/1c From this Table insert the £16.43 and £7.82.

Col 2 Insert the gross weekly pay figure (£130).

Col 3 Insert the total pay Smith has had to date (£1030).

Now open the Pay Adjustment Tables at Week 7 (middle opposite)

Col 4 As Smith's Tax Code is 344L (taken from his P45), his total "free pay" to date is £464.31.

Col 5 Now deduct £464.31 from £1030 = £565.69.

Next, refer to the Taxable Pay Tables (bottom Table opposite).

Col 6 The tax due on £565 is £125 + £16.25 = £141.25 less £16.83 (from the Subtraction Table (not shown here but is found beside Table B) and is due to the 20% tax band).

Col 7 Take £113.96 from £124.42 to get the tax due: £10.46.

NET WAGE From Smith's gross wage of £130, deduct the NIC (£7.82) and Income Tax (£10.46) to get his net wage.

Note: Tax Codes and the Tables opposite change from time to time, but the procedure remains basically the same.

Weekly Table A continued
6 April 1993 to 5 April 1994

Earnings on which employee's contributions payable 1a £	Total of employee's and employer's contributions payable 1b £	Employee's contributions payable 1c £	Employer's contributions* £	Earnings on which employee's contributions payable 1a £	Total of employee's and employer's contributions payable 1b £	Employee's contributions payable 1c £	Employer's contributions* £
86	7·04	3·06	3·90	126	15·81	7·46	8·35
87	7·97	3·95	4·02	127	15·96	7·55	8·41
88	8·11	4·04	4·07	128	16·12	7·64	8·48
89	8·25	4·13	4·12	129	16·28	7·73	8·55
90	8·38	4·22	4·16	130	16·43	7·82	8·61
91	8·52	4·31	4·21	131	16·59	7·91	8·68
92	8·65	4·40	4·25	132	16·74	8·00	8·74
93	8·79	4·49	4·30	133	16·90	8·09	8·81
94	8·93	4·58	4·35	134	17·06	8·18	8·88
95	10·97	4·67	6·30	135	17·21	8·27	8·94

TABLE A - PAY ADJUSTMENT
Week 7
May 18 to May 24

Code	Total pay adjustment to date £	Code	Total pay adjustment to date £	Code	Total pay adjustment to date £	Code	Total pay adjustment to date £	Code	Total pay adjustment to date £	Code	Total pay adjustment to date £	Code	Total pay adjustment to date £	Code	Total pay adjustment to date £	Code	Total pay adjustment to date £
41	56.42	101	137.20	161	217.98	221	298.76	281	379.54	341	460.25	391	527.59	441	594.93	491	662.20
42	57.75	102	138.53	162	219.31	222	300.09	282	380.87	342	461.65	392	528.92	442	596.26	492	663.53
43	59.15	103	139.93	163	220.64	223	301.42	283	382.20	343	462.98	393	530.25	443	597.59	493	664.93
44	60.48	104	141.26	164	222.04	224	302.75	284	383.53	344	464.31	394	531.65	444	598.92	494	666.26
45	61.81	105	142.59	165	223.37	225	304.15	285	384.93	345	465.64	395	532.98	445	600.25	495	667.59

Pages 2 and 3 tell you when to use these tables

Table B
(Tax at 25%)

Remember to use the Subtraction Tables on Page 7

Tax Due on Taxable Pay from £1 to £99				Tax Due on Taxable Pay from £100 to £23,700												
Total TAXABLE PAY to date £	Total TAX DUE to date £	Total TAXABLE PAY to date £	Total TAX DUE to date £	Total TAXABLE PAY to date £	Total TAX DUE to date £	Total TAXABLE PAY to date £	Total TAX DUE to date £	Total TAXABLE PAY to date £	Total TAX DUE to date £	Total TAXABLE PAY to date £	Total TAX DUE to date £
---	---	---	---	---	---	---	---	---	---	---	---
1	0.25	61	15.25	100	25.00	6100	1525.00	12100	3025.00	18100	4525.00
2	0.50	62	15.50	200	50.00	6200	1550.00	12200	3050.00	18200	4550.00
3	0.75	63	15.75	300	75.00	6300	1575.00	12300	3075.00	18300	4575.00
4	1.00	64	16.00	400	100.00	6400	1600.00	12400	3100.00	18400	4600.00
5	1.25	65	16.25	500	125.00	6500	1625.00	12500	3125.00	18500	4625.00
6	1.50	66	16.50	600	150.00	6600	1650.00	12600	3150.00	18600	4650.00

Using a Computer

Why are small computers so popular? It must be because they offer some benefit to the user. Using a computer in your business can help you to do certain tasks faster and thereby free some of your valuable time (and your staff's time too).

If you are new to computing, you will have to learn some of the jargon, so wherever we use jargon in this chapter (highlighted in *italics*) its meaning will be explained.

A computer system consists of 3 main parts: 1) the computer itself, complete with typewriter keyboard and *screen* (which is like a TV, although portable computers use flat screens); 2) the printer (which is sometimes lumped together with the computer and called the *hardware*) and 3) the *software*, which is the instructions to make the computer operate. Software is the collective name for all the *programs* (note the American

Installing a computer in your business will not solve fundamental problems.

spelling) your computer uses. Even the most basic computer doing the simplest task will use several different programs.

You don't need to know how to program a computer as you buy ready-made programs that will do all you require. These programs come on small *diskettes* (also called *floppies* or *disks*). Diskettes come in two sizes – 5¼ inch and 3½ inch. A computer will use one or the other size, sometimes both. Diskettes are also used to *store* (also called *back-up*) your work.

A BRIEF HISTORY
The small micro-computer or PC (Personal Computer) appeared towards the end of the 1970s. When IBM launched their PC it brought a revolution to computing. Within a few years many manufacturers were producing PC *clones* which were computers that could mimic the operations of the IBM PC, use the same software, but cost less. Not surprisingly the number of small computers used in business rose dramatically.

At that time most business software was being written for the IBM PC (and hence clones too), but then Apple produced a more "user-friendly" computer called the Apple Macintosh. This required the user to point at pictorial symbols (called *icons*) on the screen to get the computer to do things. This pointing was done by a device called a *mouse* (like a marble in a pad that you roll around the desk. It's connected to the computer and as you move the mouse, a pointer moves in unison on the screen). Many new computer users found the Apple "Mac" to be just what they needed.

Not to be outdone, PC users soon had a new program, called "Windows", which also utilised icons and a mouse. An Apple Macintosh is usually *incompatible* with a PC, that is to say a diskette from one will not work properly in the other. But today there are a number of bridging programs that allow a degree of compatibility.

Since the first edition of this book was published in 1985, the rapid technical advances in computing have included .... the move from floppy diskette-only computers to those with *hard disks* (described later); mono to full colour screens; the increasing use of the higher capacity 3½ inch diskettes; the advent of in-built modems and faxes; add-on devices like a mouse; better and faster printers; the advent of portable, then "lap-top" and now even smaller computers... and all this with an ever increasing array of software to use. In larger businesses, many small computers are now connected together in what are called *networks*.

WHAT USE IS A COMPUTER?
The tasks most commonly done by small business computer systems are:

Word Processing A computing term to describe using the computer as a clever typewriter.

Spreadsheets This program gives the computer the ability to do arithmetical calculations such as required by a Cashflow or complex invoice.

Databases In this role the computer acts like a clever filing cabinet. It can store a great deal of information that you can find, alter or print out in pre-selected groupings.

Accounts Doing your book-keeping on a computer is another very popular use. Or you may simply use a payroll program or one that prints out your invoices.

Let us look at each of the above uses:

Word Processing Unlike a typewriter that prints as you hit the keys, the computer merely remembers the keys you have touched and displays them on the screen with nothing being printed. The big advantage is you can read on the screen what you've written, add or delete words, make corrections or copy complete blocks of text previously stored in

Using a Computer

the computer memory. Then once you are happy with the document, you feed paper into the printer, hit a few buttons and it will print out the document.

The main benefit of using a computer as a word processor is where you are doing a lot of typing that uses chunks of standard text, such as repetitive letters (eg a mailshot) or preparing quotes.

There are many popular word processing programs available. Two well-known examples are WordPerfect and WordStar.

Spreadsheets In the chapter **Preparing the Business Plan**, the concept of the Cashflow Forecast was introduced. There are excellent programs that can do all the arithmetic associated with completing a cashflow. If, as is strongly recommended, you are controlling your finances by Cashflow Management techniques then each month you need to update your original Cashflow Forecast and the computer is ideally suited to this task.

This type of program can also be used for calculating and printing out complex invoices where there are many items, eg 50 metres cloth @ £8.52 per metre which would otherwise involve you in doing a lot of arithmetic.

Some spreadsheet programs, like Lotus 1-2-3, can display the results in graphical form such as a bar chart or pie chart.

Databases This is where the computer behaves like a clever filing cabinet storing details such as a customer's name, address and particulars. The program not only allows you to update these details but also allows you to print out address labels for posting mailshots, invoices, statements etc. A database program also allows you to sort its records. For instance you could ask the computer to check through its data and print out the names and addresses of all clients in a given area or all clients who are aged under 25 or whatever. This could be of particular use in analysing your customer base. But note the requirements of the Data Protection Act, which is mentioned in the chapter **Making it Legal**.

Integrated Packages The above 3 types of programs, ie word processing, spreadsheets and databases are sometimes all integrated in one program which then allows you to swop information directly from one program to another.

Simple Accounts Very basic accounting packages can be a bonus to the time-pressed small business person, provided they fully understand the program (and its limitations) and are comfortable with entering the figures by keyboard rather than writing them in an accounts book.

Payroll Even if you have only one full-time employee you need to operate the full panoply of PAYE, National Insurance contributions and Sick Pay. Just as soon as you think you know what deductions you have to make and what paperwork to complete, someone somewhere changes the rules, so you end up spending an awful lot of time just on this one non-profit making activity. This is where a payroll package could be a lifesaver, but do ensure the software house will provide updates and at a reasonable charge.

Invoicing In some businesses, producing invoices with all the calculations and discounts, VAT etc can be tedious and there is great danger of making expensive errors. A simple invoicing program can be a great help. Where your customers buy on credit, producing Statements can also be time consuming.

Full Accounts Packages

Whereas all the programs mentioned so far may be of use to any small business, however small, a full multi-ledger accounts package is mainly of benefit to a larger small business, where the sheer volume of transactions can make computerisation worthwhile. While it might take you a week or two (with a little effort) to learn to use a word processing or simple accounts program, a full accounts package may take a year or much more to implement completely.

This is partly due to the amount of data you need to type into the computer, eg stock inventory. Furthermore, the computerisation of the accounts of a business will probably give you sleepless nights and will always take much longer than you could ever anticipate when you started the project. There will also usually be ghastly errors and customers will be sent meaningless Statements (much to their annoyance). Good advice here is first, to fully understand multi-ledger book-keeping and second, run the existing ledgers in parallel with the computerised version for at least 6 months (probably up to a year). Then you may just survive the transition. The only consolation is that once you get it working properly and the bugs ironed out (and the data correct) then it will all be worthwhile as the program will give you financial information and stock control that you probably never had before and it should help you to run a more efficient and profitable business.

Note that some industries have specialised accounts packages tailored to their specific needs, eg catering, building, farming. Your trade association should be able to tell you what packages exist and how good they are.

WHICH COMPUTER TO BUY?
The main choice is between one of the many PCs and an Apple Macintosh. There is probably less business software written for the Apple Mac and hardware prices are generally higher than for PC clones, but many people like them. The best thing is to try out both a PC with "Windows" and an Apple Mac.

Using a Computer

A big mistake is to buy a computer with insufficient speed or memory capacity. Although a PC XT may be adequate for basic word processing, when you try to run more complex programs on it, they will run very slowly indeed. In terms of storage memory, whereas a 20Mb *hard-disk* was sufficient at one time, newer programs sometimes take up more space and 40Mb or more is a better bet today. (Mb is Megabyte, which is a measure of the size of computer memory and a hard-disk is where the computer stores its programs and data). You will also hear the expression *RAM* used, meaning Random Access Memory which is a transient memory that loses its information when you switch the computer off. RAM, as well as the power of the computer's processor, affects the speed with which the computer carries out its tasks. In general, the more RAM the better.

You also need to decide if you want a mono screen (this could be amber, green or black & white) or a colour screen. The latter is more expensive and some people can find the colours glaring, but more and more programs make use of the colours, so again you may find having a mono screen limiting in the future.

WHICH SOFTWARE TO BUY?

This is not an easy task as the choice is huge and each program offers different features and operates slightly differently. The various computing magazines often compare programs and you could also ask friends which programs they use. Whatever program you eventually decide on, first try to get a "demo disk" to get a feel for it yourself. A word of caution: It's all too easy to buy the wrong software and be driven to despair as a result!

Shareware This is an interesting way to evaluate and purchase programs as you get a fully working version on diskette to evaluate for £3 + VAT and carriage. If you like the program and wish to use it then you register and pay for a manual and up-to-date version of the program. In addition to main *application programs* (eg word processing), shareware is also a useful source of simple programs to help you do routine tasks. In the UK, you can purchase shareware from Shareware Marketing (tel: 0297 24088) who have a catalogue with full details.

WHICH PRINTER TO BUY?

For all applications, other than quality letter writing, the *dot matrix printer* is adequate and the cheapest, but it can be quite noisy. Most dot matrix printers can run at several speeds, the slowest speed producing what is called NLQ (Near Letter Quality) print. Note that the speed at which any printer operates is significant, and a slow printer will make you very impatient as you wait and wait for a letter to be printed! *Ink-jet* or *Bubble-jet printers* squirt ink onto the paper and cost a bit more to buy than dot matrix printers (and their ink cartridges are quite pricey) but they do produce very nice crisp black print and are quiet. Top of the range in terms of both performance and cost are the *laser printers*.

Fanfold or Cut-sheet? Some printers take continuous fanfold paper which is normally *tractor fed* (ie there are sprocket holes on each side of the paper) and cut-sheet paper (ie single sheets, like letterheads) which are normally *friction fed* (like a typewriter) and loaded either manually one at a time or by an automatic feeder. Some printers can only take cut-sheet paper. If you are using the computer for accounts purposes, then it probably needs to handle fanfold paper in addition to single sheets.

P.S. If you plan to use a computer for your accounts you should first discuss this idea with your accountant.

COMPUTER VIRUSES

The name can be a bit alarming to the uninitiated. A computer virus is simply a destructive or malicious program, it does not affect humans! However it can be a nuisance and expensive as it can wreck the data held on your computer and in some cases can even damage the computer hardware itself. There are now many hundreds, possibly thousands, of such viruses in existence.

A computer usually catches a virus from an infected diskette. Normally a blank diskette or a program diskette from a reliable manufacturer should not be infected. Another way your computer can catch a virus is over a modem.

Precautions:

1. Back-up your work at least daily on diskettes. (This is good practice anyway as sometimes computers break down or there is a power cut and you can lose what work you have done).

2. Do hard copy back-ups (ie paper print-outs) regularly.

3. Be very wary of using diskettes from friends – use only new blank diskettes or program diskettes purchased from reliable sources.

4. Avoid using free diskettes if possible.

5. Minimise use of modems and only connect to reliable parties.

6. Consider buying an anti-virus program.

IN CONCLUSION

There are many types of computer on the market and even more varieties of software. Most will do the job adequately but before you decide to buy a particular system try it out fully doing precisely the tasks you will use it for, including printing. Remember to ask the supplier what back-up they can give if you hit a snag with a program or there is some fault with the computer hardware■

Learning from Failures

The purpose of this short chapter is simple — to give a number of actual case histories (omitting the company names) which illustrate clearly the most common reasons for small businesses failing, particularly in their first few years. It is said that it takes 3 to 5 years for a business to become "established". You will, I hope, notice from the examples below that the primary cause of business failures is poor management and is therefore avoidable!

Under-financed   A small manufacturing firm produced a car accessory for which there would have been a good demand. Unfortunately it was a very novel device and a significant promotional campaign would have been needed to "educate" the consumer. The firm did not have the necessary resources to mount the required promotional campaign and so the product died.

Note: Far too many businesses start with inadequate finance. They struggle for a short period then collapse. When preparing the Cashflow Forecast, do not underestimate your cash requirements.

Over-gearing (This describes the situation when a firm's borrowings are disproportionate to its capital). A manufacturing firm employing 20 people was set up with only ¼ of the start-up capital being provided by the investors as share capital, the remainder being loans. The business collapsed after several years and one key factor was the burden of interest payments.

Low Pricing   A small health food shop opened near an existing shop (several hundred yards down the same street) hoping to enter the market by selling everything at a lower price than the original shop. The original shop wisely kept its prices unchanged and the new shop collapsed within a year, unable to meet its overheads with its low profit mark-up.

Note: Most new businesses tend to under price.

Partnership Problems   A grocery shop was set up by 3 partners (but no Partnership Agreement). The shop was performing adequately but one partner chose to leave and the remaining partners bought the outgoing partner's share by raising a bank loan and paying off the partner immediately. The heavy interest charges and capital repayments began to have serious effects on the shop and one

partner took ill leaving the last partner to carry the entire burden ... until the inevitable ending.

Note: There should have been a Partnership Agreement and in this context it should have allowed for: a) Retirement of Partners — the purchase of his share by an amount to be paid in instalments over at least one year and b) in the event of illness a partnership can be dissolved.

Insufficient Financial Control This is probably the most common type of failure so there are two examples ... A service business was primarily involved in £20,000 + contracts which took many weeks to complete. The company took no records of the man-hours spent on each contract. Furthermore their accounts were always made up many months in arrears. It was too late for the company when their accountants spotted the fundamental problem in that each contract was costing the company more than they had quoted so they were actually trading at a loss!

Insufficient financial control ...

Another company, this time a furniture manufacturer, was "operating" a set of accounts books that were so complex that even the Managing Director did not understand them and second, they were always hopelessly out of date. The company slipped ever more into the red and to make matters worse the company paid little heed to its overdraft limit and kept writing cheques until the bank started to bounce them. This caused the company's trade suppliers to remove the credit they were giving thereby compounding

Learning from Failures

the problem whereupon the bank felt the whole matter was out of control and threatened to withdraw the overdraft.

Note: Another variety of poor financial control is *overspending* which manifests itself in a number of ways — purchasing excessive amounts of stock, buying expensive machinery or office equipment which are under utilised, acquiring new cars for Directors and buying new equipment when it could have been purchased second-hand.

Excessive Overheads A successful company after trading for several years noticed its overdraft level steadily mounting. The increase did not seem to be related to expansion and instead there was decreasing profitability. The cause was found to be rising overheads out of proportion to the turnover of the business, in particular there were too many staff with too many "hangers-on"!

Note: By proper Cashflow Management this would have been noticed earlier.

... in particular there were too many staff.

Over-trading (This phrase describes a company expanding more rapidly than its available working capital allows). A small electronics company found its products in great demand so bought more raw materials and took on more staff to meet the expanding order book. This increased the company's borrowings until it was bouncing along its overdraft limit and at times had difficulty even in paying its staff (this situation is also often referred to as "having cashflow problems").

Note: This is to some extent related to "Under-financed" in that provision for expansion should have been made in the initial start-up budget. Alternatively the firm should now negotiate a re-financing package with its investors and bank. Companies that are over-trading are very vulnerable as they have no spare cash to meet contingencies or competition.

Insufficient Trade This is almost the opposite to "Over-trading". Since it affects so many companies in so many industrial sectors, no specific case history is necessary here. It can affect large companies as equally as small ones. If you are operating a good Cashflow Management system you will soon be aware that your level of trading is too low. The following corrective actions can then be considered: (a) increase marketing effort; (b) induce sales by special promotions, sales, discounts; (c) consider moving into new markets, possibly in new geographical areas; (d) think of diversification and (e) analyse your sales staff's techniques and records to spot problems. Finally, reduce your overheads until they can be supported by your cashflow and if there is really no hope, quit while you still can.

Internal Theft A new restaurant was opened by an inexperienced restaurateur who had little knowledge of the behind-the-scenes goings on. The restaurant ceased trading within 12 months. A significant factor was the high level of theft of food and drink by staff.

Note: The catering and licensed trades are particularly vulnerable to the problem, but proprietors of *all* businesses need to be continually alert to this serious problem.

Eggs-In-One-Basket A successful magazine publishing concern distributed all its magazines, apart from those on direct subscription, through a distributor which is normal practice. Unfortunately the distributor collapsed owing the

Learning from Failures

publisher for the last two copies of the magazine with the net result that the publishing company itself was forced into liquidation.

Note: The same situation can occur with sub-contract companies when a disproportionate amount of their business is with one customer. A remedy is to keep a close eye on the company you are dealing with and to ensure they make regular (and prompt) payments.

New Product Introduction A specialist car manufacturer (they in fact produced a stylish glassfibre bodied sports-car that was mated to Ford running gear) enjoyed such great success with their car that they started to design and develop a second, more sophisticated, model. As happens so frequently the company underestimated both the costs and delays associated with this new car and it was a major factor in the demise of the company.

Note: Engineers frequently underestimate the cost and timescale of designing and developing a new or improved product – with potentially fatal results. However it is important for all manufacturers to have new products in the pipeline and the timing of their development and launch is crucial.

Milking (This phrase describes the action of a proprietor when he withdraws an excessive amount of money from a business). A computer services company was first in the field and so made substantial profits but little of this was retained in the business. Eventually the company was confronted by well-funded competitors who were anxious to "muscle in" on the market and the original company did not have the financial strength to fight back.

Note: A common and silly example of milking is the person who sets up a company, becomes a "Director" for the first time, and promptly buys himself a new car – just at the crucial stage of setting up the new firm, when it probably needs to retain every pound it can. Most entrepreneurs have to sacrifice a good deal over many years before they achieve success and it is important that as much of the profits as possible are "ploughed back" into the company.

Lack of Initial Planning A redundant truck driver was offered a second-hand truck at a bargain price so thought he would set up a one-man haulage/delivery business. His very first action was to buy the truck! No market research,

however simple, was done and in fact there was no local market which could have used that type of truck (which was why it was up for sale in the first place!).

LEARNING ...

Failure is as much a part of business as success. Even large successful companies make awful mistakes and some of their ventures are complete and utter failures – the difference between them and you is they can usually *afford* the failures! By remembering the different cases given above you may hopefully spot any similar trend in your own business and take corrective action early enough to recover.

Finally, there is no such thing in business as easy or quick profit nor does simply long hours and effort achieve results – it is a combination of thought, preparation and application. Starting a business is relatively easy – it is staying in business that is the real challenge ■

You've read the book, had the dreams, now start the business ...

Getting more Business Advice

Accountants   An accountant is an essential part of your team. Accountants vary greatly in their abilities and in the time they are prepared to spend with each client. A poor or uninterested accountant can even be contributory to the demise of a business – so choose carefully! An initial meeting with an accountant is usually free. Discuss your business plans, what accounts books you plan to keep and ask for an indication of likely annual fees. An accountant should always be consulted when setting up a business and later to help you with your annual Tax Return. It is important that you get on with your accountant and keep in touch.

Bank Managers   A Bank Manager's advice is usually free and you should keep them abreast of all developments and plans. They are careful people so do not frighten them with sudden changes of course and do not give them ultimatums such as "If I don't get the £5,000 overdraft tomorrow, I shall have to lay off my staff..". Give them warning. You should visit your bank manager or at least phone or write to them every few months just to keep in touch. Many bankers have more business knowledge than you might expect, but as with any service if you are unhappy with your bank, then consider changing branch or to another bank. But do remember it is usually worth staying with the bank who know you.

Chartered Surveyors   Always use a chartered surveyor when purchasing premises or taking on a lease (ie renting). They can check on the physical condition of the building, advise if the rent or purchase price is fair and they can check and advise on the lease conditions and planning permission. They will charge for their service so ask them for an estimate beforehand.

Enterprise Agencies   Enterprise Agencies are usually funded jointly by the local Private and Public sectors which allows them to provide most of their services free of charge. The objective of the 300 Enterprise Agencies is to encourage new and existing small businesses, providing mainly free business advice and much more besides. To find your nearest, look in the Yellow Pages. Alternatively in England, Wales or Northern Ireland, contact Business In The Community at 8 Stratton Street, London W1X 5FD, tel: 071-629 1600. Fax: 071-629 1834.
   In Scotland, contact Scottish Business In The Community at Romano House, 43 Station Road, Corstorphine, Edinburgh EH12 7AF, tel: 031-334 9876. Fax: 031-316 4521.

Industrial Development Units   Many local authorities have such units. They can provide business advice and usually have factory premises to rent. They can also advise on local planning and licencing matters.

Local Enterprise Companies (LECs)   These are business-led organisations in Scotland, formed to encourage enterprise, provide training and assist small firms, in addition to other related activities. Get the address of your own LEC from Scottish Enterprise (see below) or Yellow Pages.

Solicitors   A good solicitor is needed when setting up a business, taking over premises or whenever you have legal queries.

Training and Enterprise Councils (TECs) These are business-led organisations in England and Wales, formed to encourage enterprise, provide training and assist small firms, in addition to other related activities. Get the address of your own TEC from a JobCentre or Yellow Pages.

And Finally   Remember that advice is not a substitute for decision making! Collect all the advice you can but in the end you must make your own decisions.

USEFUL ADDRESSES

**Highlands and Islands Enterprise
(includes Orkney & Shetland)**
Bridge House, 20 Bridge Street, Inverness IV1 1QR
Tel: 0463 234171. Fax: 0463 244469

Scottish Enterprise
120 Bothwell Street, Glasgow G2 7JP
Tel: 041-248 2700. Fax: 041-221 3217

Scottish Business Shop
(same address) Tel: 041-248 6014

Local Enterprise Development Unit (LEDU)
Ledu House, Upper Galwally, Belfast BT8 4TB
Tel: 0232 491031. Fax: 0232 691432

Welsh Development Agency (WDA)
Pearl House, Greyfriars Road, Cardiff CF1 3XX
Tel: 0222 222666. Fax: 0222 390752

Development Board for Rural Wales
Ladywell House, Newtown, Powys SY16 1JB
Tel: 0686 626965. Fax: 0686 627889

Rural Development Commission
141 Castle Street, Salisbury, Wiltshire SP1 3TP
Tel: 0722 336255. Fax: 0722 332769

Federation of Small Businesses
140 Lower Marsh, Westminster Bridge, London SE1 7AE
Tel: 071-928 9272. Fax: 071-401 2544

Tax Data Page

Note 1: The figures and rates of tax quoted on this page reflect the November 1993 Budget proposals for 1994/95.

Note 2: To ensure you have correct and up-to-date information, please check with the relevant tax authorities.

Income Tax

Basic Rate: 25% (but the first £3,000 of taxable income is taxed at 20%)

Higher Rate: 40% (for that portion of taxable income exceeding £23,700)

Personal Allowances:

Single Person:	£3,445	
Married Couple:	£1,720 additional allowance	
Single Parent:	£1,720 additional allowance	

What this means is a single unmarried person with no children will have a personal allowance of £3,445. If that person has dependent children there is an additional £1,720 allowance making £5,165 in total. A married couple (with only one person working) have a total allowance of £5,165. With both partners working their combined allowance is £8,610. Note that a husband and wife are taxed independently.

PAYE: Lower Limit: £66.50 per week or £288 per month (ie there is normally no Income Tax to be deducted if an employee's wage is likely to be less than this figure – this limit is mainly relevant to part-time staff).

Simple Tax Accounts If your annual turnover does not exceed £15,000, the Inland Revenue will accept simplified "three line accounts" which provide a summary of: (1) turnover, (2) total business expenditure and (3) your profits. Get leaflet IR104 for more information.

National Insurance

Class 1 (Employees/Directors) — Lower Limit: £57 weekly or £247 monthly (ie there is normally no National Insurance contribution (or Employers contribution) on earnings below this limit).

Class 1A (Cars and Fuel) — This is a contribution (only by Employers) if cars are made available for private use to their Employees or Directors. It is assessed according to a "scale charge".

Class 2 (Sole Traders/Partners) — £5.65 per week. (The Small Earnings Exception limit is £3,200 per annum).

Class 4 (Sole Traders/Partners) — Calculated as 7.3% of profits between £6,490 and £22,360, ie no Class 4 contribution due if taxable profits are under £6,490.

Corporation Tax
(Limited Companies only)

The tax rate is 25% for profits up to £300,000. This is called the "small companies' rate". Thereafter the tax rate rises to a maximum of 33%.

Value Added Tax (VAT)

Standard Rate: 17½%   Registration threshold: £45,000 (turnover)

Capital Gains Tax (CGT)

Annual exemption: First £5,800 of chargeable gain.

INDEX